W9-ATR-300

# THE FAMILY READ-ALOUD
# HOLIDAY TREASURY

Franklin Pierce
Law Center
N.H. 03301

# THE FAMILY READ-ALOUD
# HOLIDAY
# TREASURY

FRANKLIN PIERCE
COLLEGE LIBRARY
RINDGE, N.H. 03461

## SELECTED BY ALICE LOW
## ILLUSTRATED BY MARC BROWN

JOY STREET BOOKS

LITTLE, BROWN AND COMPANY
BOSTON TORONTO LONDON

*For Steve and Sue, Diego and Ilean, Rod and Helen*
*and Jesse and Julie, with love.*
A.L.

*With love to Eliza Morgan Brown*
*who gets the first book as promised*
M.B.

CURR
PN
6071
. H7
F3
1991

Text selection copyright © 1991 by Alice Low
Illustrations copyright © 1991 by Marc Brown
All rights reserved. No part of this book may be reproduced in any form or by any electronic or
mechanical means, including information storage and retrieval systems, without permission in writing from the publisher, except by a reviewer, who may quote brief passages in a review.

First edition

Acknowledgments begin on page 153.

ISBN 0-316-53368-8
Library of Congress Catalog Card Number: 91-53174
Library of Congress Cataloging-in-Publication information is available.

Joy Street Books are published by
Little, Brown and Company (Inc.)

10 9 8 7 6 5 4 3 2 1

AG-TN
Book design by Sylvia Frezzolini

Published simultaneously in Canada by
Little, Brown and Company (Canada) Limited

Printed in the United States of America

# CONTENTS

# Celebrating Me

## ME I AM

I am the only ME I AM who qualifies as me; no ME I AM has been before, and none will ever be.

No other ME I AM can feel the feelings I've within; no other ME I AM can fit precisely in my skin.

There is no other ME I AM who thinks the thoughts I do; the world contains one ME I AM, there is no room for two.

I am the only ME I AM this earth shall ever see; that ME I AM I always am is no one else but ME!

ANONYMOUS

## DREAM VARIATIONS

To fling my arms wide
In some place of the sun,
To whirl and to dance
Till the white day is done.
Then rest at cool evening
Beneath a tall tree
While night comes on gently,
  Dark like me—
That is my dream!

To fling my arms wide
In the face of the sun,
Dance! Whirl! Whirl!
Till the quick day is done.
Rest at pale evening . . .
A tall, slim tree . . .
Night coming tenderly
  Black like me.

LANGSTON HUGHES

## MY OWN DAY

When I opened my eyes this morning,
The day belonged to me.
The sky was mine and the sun,
And my feet got up dancing.
The marmalade was mine and the squares of sidewalk
And all the birds in the trees.
So I stood and I considered
Stopping the world right there,
Making today go on and on forever.
But I decided not to.
I let the world spin on and I went to school.
I almost did it, but then, I said to myself,
"Who knows what you might be missing tomorrow?"

JEAN LITTLE

3

# New Year's Day

BEGINNING A NEW YEAR MEANS

taking off
  clothes spattered with
  chocolate milk
  and mud
throwing away
  scribbled pages
  full of crossed out words
  and mistakes
watching
  old snow
  melting away

putting on
  clean clothes
  without spots or wrinkles
opening
  white pages
  with nothing written
  on them yet
watching
  fresh snow
  falling
  without tiremarks
  or footprints

RUTH WHITMAN

## CHINESE NEW YEAR

You'll find whenever the New Year comes
The Kitchen God will want some plums.
The girls will want some flowers new;
The boys will want firecrackers, too.
A new felt cap will please papa,
And a sugar cake for dear mama.

TRADITIONAL CHINESE NURSERY RHYME

## BOUQUET OF ROSES

A bouquet of roses,
A bouquet of roses,
From this flowering bush;
Hark! The New Year's coming
And the old one's gone.

Olive tree, I'm leaving,
Olive tree, I'm leaving,
For the olive grove;
Hark! The New Year's coming
And the old one's gone.

TRADITIONAL PUERTO RICAN SONG

## TRAIGO UN RAMILLETE

Traigo un ramillete,
traigo un ramillete
de un lindo rosal,
un año que viene
y otro que se va.

Vengo del olivo,
vengo del olivo,
voy pa'l olivar
un año que viene
y otro que se va.

5

# Martin Luther King Day

WE SHALL OVERCOME

We shall overcome,
We shall overcome,
We shall overcome some day.
Oh, here in my heart
I do believe
We shall overcome someday.

We can build a new world,
We can build a new world,
We can build a new world some day.
Oh, here in my heart
I do believe
We can build a new world someday.

We can walk in peace,
We can walk in peace,
We can walk in peace one day.
Oh, here in my heart
I do believe
We can walk in peace one day.

ZILPHIA HORTON,
FRANK HAMILTON,
GUY CARAWAN,
AND PETE SEEGER

## DREAMS

Hold fast to dreams
For if dreams die
Life is a broken-winged bird
That cannot fly.

Hold fast to dreams
For when dreams go
Life is a barren field
Frozen with snow.

LANGSTON HUGHES

# Valentine's Day

### THE OWL AND THE PUSSYCAT

The Owl and the Pussycat went to sea
    In a beautiful pea-green boat;
They took some honey, and plenty of money
    Wrapped up in a five-pound note.
The Owl looked up to the stars above,
    And sang to a small guitar,
"O, lovely Pussy! O, Pussy, my love,
    What a beautiful Pussy you are,
        You are,
        You are!
What a beautiful Pussy you are!"

Pussy said to the Owl, "You elegant fowl!
    How charmingly sweet you sing!
Oh! let us be married; too long we have tarried:
    But what shall we do for a ring?"
They sailed away, for a year and a day,
    To the land where the bong-tree grows;
And there in a wood a Piggy-wig stood
    With a ring at the end of his nose,
        His nose,
        His nose,
With a ring at the end of his nose.

"Dear Pig, are you willing to sell for one shilling
    Your ring?" Said the Piggy, "I will."
So they took it away, and were married next day
    By the Turkey who lives on the hill.
They dined on mince and slices of quince,
    Which they ate with a runcible spoon,
And hand in hand, on the edge of the sand,
    They danced by the light of the moon,
        The moon,
        The moon,
They danced by the light of the moon.

EDWARD LEAR

8

## REBUS VALENTINE

You may not  all for me

   The way I care for you.

You may  your nose

   When I plead with you—

But if your  should  with mine

   Forever  hope

There is no reason in the world

   Why we two

ANONYMOUS

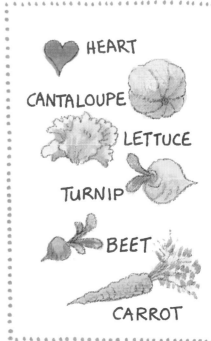

HEART
CANTALOUPE
LETTUCE
TURNIP
BEET
CARROT

---

## I MADE MY DOG A VALENTINE

I made my dog a valentine,
she sniffed it very hard,
then chewed on it a little while
and left it in the yard.

I made one for my parrakeets,
a pretty paper heart,
they pulled it with their claws
   and beaks
until it ripped apart.

I made one for my turtle,
all *he* did was get it wet,
I wonder if a valentine
is wasted on a pet.

JACK PRELUTSKY

I love you,
I love you,
I love you
 so well,
If I had a
 peanut,
I'd give you
 the shell.

ANONYMOUS

## The Porcupine

A porcupine looks somewhat silly,
He also is extremely quilly
And if he shoots a quill at you
Run fast
Or you'll be quilly too.

I would not want a porcupine
To be my loving valentine.

KARLA KUSKIN

# Presidents' Day

### ABRAHAM LINCOLN

Lincoln was a long man.
He liked out of doors.
He liked the wind blowing
And the talk in country stores.

He liked telling stories,
He liked telling jokes.
"Abe's quite a character,"
Said quite a lot of folks.

Lots of folks in Springfield
Saw him every day,
Walking down the street
In his gaunt, long way.

Shawl around his shoulders,
Letters in his hat.
"That's Abe Lincoln."
They thought no more than that.

Knew that he was honest,
Guessed that he was odd,
Knew he had a cross wife
Though she was a Todd.

Knew he had three little boys
Who liked to shout and play,
Knew he had a lot of debts
It took him years to pay.

Knew his clothes and knew his house.
"That's his office, here.
Blame good lawyer, on the whole,
Though he's sort of queer.

"Sure he went to Congress, once,
But he didn't stay.
Can't expect us all to be
Smart as Henry Clay.

"Need a man for troubled times?
Well, I guess we do.
Wonder who we'll ever find?
Yes—I wonder who."

That is how they met and talked,
Knowing and unknowing.
Lincoln was the green pine.
Lincoln kept on growing.

ROSEMARY CARR AND STEPHEN VINCENT BENÉT

13

## GEORGE WASHINGTON'S BREAKFAST

JEAN FRITZ

George W. Allen was proud of two things. His name and his birthday.

George was named for George Washington. And he had the same birthday. February 22.

It made him feel almost related, he said.

It made him want to know everything there was to know about George Washington.

Already he knew quite a lot. He knew that Washington was a general and lived in Virginia and was six feet tall and married to Martha and was the first President of the United States.

He knew that Washington rode two horses in the war, Blueskin and Nelson, but Nelson was his favorite because he was so steady in gunfire.

He also knew that Washington once had ten hunting dogs. Their names were: Tipsey, Pompey, Harry, Maiden, Lady, Dutchess, Drunkard, Tru-Love, Mopsy, and Pilot.

Then one day at breakfast George Allen thought of something he didn't know. George's mother and father had gone to work, and his grandmother was frying eggs.

"Grandma," George said, "what did George Washington eat for breakfast?"

"Search me," his grandmother said. "That was before my time."

George's grandmother knew what George was like. When George wanted to find out something, he didn't rest until he found out. He didn't let anyone else rest either. He did just what his grandfather used to do—ask questions, collect books, and pester everyone for answers. And George's grandmother wasn't going to fool around now about breakfasts that were over and done with two hundred years ago.

"Well," he said, "if I find out, will you do one thing for me?"

"What's that?"

"Will you cook me George Washington's breakfast?"

George's grandmother looked at the clock on the kitchen wall. "George," she said, "you'll be late for school."

"But will you?" George insisted. "Will you cook me George Washington's breakfast?"

George's grandmother was still looking at the clock. "I'll cook anything," she said, "as long as you hurry."

After school that day George Allen went to the library.

"Miss Willing," he said to the librarian, "do you know what George Washington ate for breakfast?"

Miss Willing could hardly remember what *she'd* had for breakfast that morning, but like George, she liked to find out.

Together George and Miss Willing went to the encyclopedia and looked under *W*. "Washington, George." The encyclopedia said Washington was born in 1732, married in 1759, elected President in 1789 and died in 1799. It told all about the years when he took trips and fought battles and did other important things. But it didn't say what he did everyday. It didn't mention his breakfasts.

Miss Willing took George to the card catalogue. There were seven books about George Washington. Most of them were in the section of the library marked *B* for Biography.

George picked out four books to take home, and Miss Willing promised that she would look at the rest.

That night after supper George gave his father a book to read, and he gave his mother a book to read.

"Don't look at me," his grandmother said. "I'll cook but I won't look."

So George kept the other two books for himself. All evening George and his mother and father read.

George was very excited when he found out that Washington liked to count things. George liked to count things too. George had counted how many steps there were between his house and the school. And there was Washington back in the 1700's counting steps too! It made George feel more related than ever.

The book said that once Washington figured out that there were 71,000 seeds in a pound of red clover. And 844,800 seeds in a pound of Red River grass.

But there wasn't a word about Washington's breakfasts, and the way George figured it, Washington must have eaten breakfast more than 24,000 times.

Then all at once Mrs. Allen looked up. "Listen to this," she said. "This book says that in Washington's time breakfast in Virginia usually consisted of cold turkey, cold meat, fried hominy, toast, cider, ham, bread and butter, tea, coffee and chocolate."

George Allen felt his mouth beginning to water. He grinned and looked at his grandmother.

"Humph!" his grandmother scoffed. "Notice the book said what was *usual* in Virginia. Everyone knows George Washington was an unusual man. No telling what he ate."

A little later Mr. Allen looked up from his book. "Guess what?" he said. "It says here that people in Washington's day didn't eat a real breakfast. Instead they had lunch at ten o'clock in the morning."

George Allen's grandmother grinned and looked at George.

"Doesn't mean a thing," George said. "That book's talking about Washington's day. Not about George Washington."

George went back to the library. Miss Willing suggested that they find out what some of George Washington's friends had to say.

First they read from the diary of John Adams, who was the second President of the United States. John Adams wrote that George Washington ruined his teeth when he was a boy by cracking walnuts in his mouth.

Thomas Jefferson, the third President of the United States, wrote that Washington was the best horseman of his age.

General Lafayette, who helped Washington fight the Revolutionary War, wrote that George Washington wore a size 13 shoe and had the biggest hands he'd ever seen. It was said that he could bend a horseshoe with his bare hands.

No one mentioned if George Washington ever ate or not.

Day after day George and his mother and father and Miss Willing read. Then one day Miss Willing said the reading was over. There were no more books in the library about George Washington. Of course there were bigger libraries, she pointed out. George could go to one of them.

But George had a different idea. "We'll go to Washington's home in Mount Vernon, Virginia," he said, "where George Washington's breakfasts were actually cooked."

The next weekend George and Mr. and Mrs. Allen got into the car. They asked George's grandmother to come, but she said no.

On the way to Mount Vernon, George and his mother and father stopped at Washington, D.C. George wanted to go to the Smithsonian Institution, a museum that had all kinds of historical exhibits.

"You won't find George Washington's breakfast here," Mr. Allen said. "He ate his breakfasts. He didn't put them in a glass case."

George didn't expect to see George Washington himself, and he certainly didn't expect to see him dressed in a curtain. George's father said that Washington was wearing a Roman toga. Not that he had ever worn a Roman toga, but the sculptor thought he'd look nice in it.

George did see the uniform that Washington wore on December 23, 1783, when he resigned from the Army. It was a black and tan uniform, and it had white ruffles and brass buttons. Every place George looked there were brass buttons—down the front of the jacket, on the vest, at the back of the neck, on the sleeves and pockets, on the tails of the coat and at the knees. George walked all around the uniform and counted the buttons. There were 64 brass buttons.

Then George walked back to the statue. "I bet you and I," he said, "are the only ones in the world who ever counted up all those buttons."

At Mount Vernon George and his mother and father went right into the kitchen. They walked on the same path that Washington had walked on, and every time George put his feet down, he thought of Washington's size 13's in the same spot.

The kitchen was in a separate building at the side of the house. It was a large room with a brick fireplace at one end and brass pots and

iron pots and griddles and pans and ladles hanging on the walls. George held his breath. It was at that very fireplace, he told himself, that Washington's breakfasts had been cooked. The food may actually have been in some of those very pots and pans. Suddenly George felt so related to Washington that goose pimples broke out on his arm.

He turned to a guard in uniform standing at the door. "Can you tell me," George said, "what George Washington ate for breakfast?"

The guard spoke as if he were reciting a lesson. "Breakfast was at seven. The guests were served tea and coffee and meat, both cold and boiled."

"And did Washington eat the same breakfast?" The guard looked confused. "I don't know," he said, "I've only been here eight months."

On Sunday afternoon George and his father and mother went home. They found George's grandmother and Miss Willing waiting together on the front porch.

"No luck," George reported.

Mr. Allen put his hand on George's shoulder. "It was a good try, son," he said. "You can't win them all."

"Sometimes there's nothing to do but give up," Mrs. Allen said.

George Allen looked at his family in amazement. *"Give up!"* he shouted. "You expect me to give up! George Washington's soldiers were starving, and they didn't give up. They were freezing, and they didn't give up. *What do you think I am?"*

George was so mad he slammed the screen door and went up to his room. But even upstairs he could hear them talking to Miss Willing about him. George stamped up to the attic. It was quiet here. And very neat. He could see his grandmother had been working.

Next to him was a box filled with things he guessed his grandmother meant to throw away. On top of the box was an old stuffed dog. One ear was torn now, but still, he was a good dog. George put him aside.

He looked back in the box. There was a bunch of old Batman comics. It was a good thing he'd come up here, he thought. No one should throw away old comics.

Under the comics George found a book. It was an old book, and beat-up-looking—probably his grandfather's, he thought, and it seemed a shame to throw it away. The *American Miracle*, the book was called, and it was written by the honorable Samuel Stearns, whoever he was.

George whistled as he turned the pages. The honorable Samuel Stearns thought he knew everything. He told you how to choose a wife, how to kill bedbugs and how to keep from getting bald. He named the birds of North America (140), and he listed all the famous earthquakes since the year 17 (63 earthquakes). Then there was a chapter called "The Character of Washington."

George looked back at the title page where he knew he would find the date that the book was published.

"1791," he read. Samuel Stearns was living at the same time as Washington.

George turned back to the chapter on Washington. "Well, Mr. Stearns," George said, "if you know so much, kindly inform me about Washington's breakfast."

"Washington," Mr. Stearns wrote, "raised 7,000 bushels of wheat and 10,000 bushels of corn in one year."

"Okay, okay," George said. "That wasn't the question."

"Washington," Mr. Stearns continued, "is very regular, temperate, and industrious; rises winter and summer at dawn of day."

"Then what?" George asked.

"He breakfasts about seven," Mr. Stearns wrote, "on . . . ."

Suddenly George let out a whoop. He put the book behind his back and clattered down the steps.

"Grandma!" he shouted. "When did you say you'd cook me George Washington's breakfast?"

"Boy, if you ever find out about that breakfast, I'll cook it right then no matter what time it is."

"Right this minute, for instance?"

"That's what I said."

George grinned. "Grandma," he said, "put on your apron." He brought the book out from behind his back.

"Washington," he read, "breakfasts about seven o'clock on three small Indian hoecakes and as many dishes of tea."

George passed the book around, and he thought he'd never seen people act as happy. All but his grandmother.

"George," she said, "I don't have the slightest idea what an Indian hoecake is."

George went to the dictionary. He looked under *H*. "Hoe-cake. A cake of cornmeal and water and salt baked before an open fire or in the ashes, originally on a hoe."

George's grandmother put on her apron. "I've cornmeal and water and salt," she said. "I guess I can make some Indian hoecakes."

George's father built a fire in the fireplace.

George's mother filled the kettle with water for the tea.

George said he'd go down to the basement for a hoe, but his grandmother stopped him. "You don't want me to cook these things on a hoe, do you?" she asked.

"That's what the dictionary says."

"The dictionary says originally. That means when hoecakes first came out. I expect they'd been around quite a while before Washington's time."

George wasn't sure. He wanted to do it right.

"Did you see a hoe in Washington's kitchen?"

George admitted there was no hoe there.

"All right then," his grandmother said. "Did you see any black iron griddles?"

George said that he had.

"That's what we'll use," his grandmother said. She mixed cornmeal and water in a bowl; she added salt; then she shaped the mixture in her hands to form little cakes.

Everyone sat around the fire to wait for breakfast. Pretty soon the tea kettle began to steam and the hoecakes began to turn a nice golden brown.

Then George's grandmother served George Washington's breakfast.

George took a bite of hoecake. It was pretty good, he thought. He looked at his mother and his father and his grandmother and Miss Willing all eating hoecakes together on a Sunday afternoon. George decided he felt more related to Washington than he'd ever felt in his whole life. It was as if George Washington were right there at the fireplace with them.

22

There was only one trouble.

When George finished his three small hoecakes and his three cups of tea, he was still hungry. And if he was hungry, he thought, what about Washington? For a man who was six feet tall and the Father of His Country, it seemed like a skimpy breakfast.

"I hope Washington didn't have long to wait until lunch," he said. "I hope he had a nice big lunch to look forward to. A nice big one. I wonder what—"

But George never finished his sentence. His grandmother was standing up.

"George Washington Allen," she cried. "Don't you *dare*!" And she pointed her spatula at him.

"Not today," Miss Willing said. "The library is closed today."

"Okay." George grinned. "Not today."

# St. Patrick's Day

## THE HUNGRY LEPRECHAUN

MARY CALHOUN

Once upon a time, and a very hard time it was, too, everyone in Ireland was poor. The Irish ground was so poor it grew little but rocks and dandelions. Young Patrick O'Michael O'Sullivan O'Callahan was so poor he had only dandelion soup to eat. Even the leprechauns were poor, not a pot of gold amongst them. But Patrick O'Michael O'Sullivan O'Callahan didn't know that. He believed in leprechaun magic, and he believed that if only he could catch a leprechaun, he'd be rich. He'd make the little man give him his gold. So every day when young Patrick went out to dig dandelions for dinner, he watched sharply for a stray leprechaun.

Now the littlest of all little men lived in a cave under the hill by Patrick's house. His name was Tippery, and he was very, *very* hungry. One day, much as he feared to, he came out in broad daylight looking for something to eat. And it happened that Patrick O'Michael was nearby, digging his dandelions. Quick, sharp! he spied the little man. And quick, jump! he flopped his hat over the creature. He'd caught him! Patrick O'Michael O'Sullivan O'Callahan had caught himself a leprechaun!

"Give me your gold, or I'll never let you go," ordered Patrick, all eager and gay.

24

"I haven't any gold, no more than you," said Tippery, all miserable and hungry. "Are dandelions good for eating?"

Then Patrick O'Michael peeked under his hat, and he saw that he'd caught the thinnest, the weakest, the most hungry-looking leprechaun that ever lived.

"Dandelion soup is better than nothing at all," he told Tippery. "I'll take you home and feed you some."

Tippery's long, narrow ears perked up when he saw his bowl of dandelion soup. He sniffed it with his round nose. And then he lapped it up with his pointed tongue. But Patrick O'Michael O'Sullivan O'Callahan still believed in leprechaun magic, and he cried, "Whoever heard of a leprechaun with no magic to make gold! For shame!"

Tippery's long ears drooped. He'd used up most of his magic in the hard times.

"Come now, where do you keep your magic?" Patrick insisted. "In your pocket? In your left shoe?"

"In my fingertips, of course," said the leprechaun. "But I was saving my wee bit for the worst time of all."

"Oho!" Young Patrick sprang up. "That worst time has come, my little man. I command you to turn this pot of dandelion soup into gold!"

"I'm still hungry," Tippery complained. "Will you make more soup if I do?"

Patrick agreed.

Now changing the soup into gold was stirring magic. But what to stir with? It had been so long since Tippery had made magic that he'd almost forgotten how. He screwed up his nose to think, and he pulled his left ear. He blew on his fingers to warm up the magic. Then he stirred the soup with the feather from his cap. But the dandelion soup only spit at him.

"Maybe—" said Tippery. He stirred the soup with a broomstraw—and the dandelions curled up.

"Or was it—?" said Tippery. He hung over the edge of the pot and stirred with his long left ear. The dandelion soup rumbled and roiled. The dandelions disappeared. Tippery had a potful of—frogs! Little green frogs hopping about. Tippery's ears hung down.

"I forgot how to make stirring magic," he said. "Let's dig dandelions and make some more soup."

"No, no. Have faith. You can do it," urged Patrick O'Michael. He pointed to the yellow puddle of sunlight on the floor.

"Sure now, you can change that into purest gold," he said.

That was sprinkling magic. But what to sprinkle with? The leprechaun bit his pointed tongue, and he pulled his right ear. He dibbled his magic fingers in the puddle of sunlight. Then he sprinkled it with ashes from the hearth. The sunlight grew runny.

"It's coming, it's coming!" shouted Patrick O'Michael.

Suddenly it turned into a puddle of water. Hop, skip, quicker than jump! The frogs were in the puddle, splashing happily.

Tippery slunk under the table, but Patrick hauled him out.

"Try once more," he begged.

By this time Tippery had used up all of his magic except what was in one little finger. Besides, he was very, *very* hungry. "Let's dig dandelions first," he said.

So Patrick and Tippery went out to the fields and dug dandelions. When they had a big pile, young Patrick pointed to all the rocks in the field.

"If only you could change those rocks into gold," he said.

That was touching magic, hardest kind of all. Tippery had to get the magic in his little finger lined up just right and—there was something he couldn't remember. "Oh well," said Tippery.

He grabbed both ears and whirled around three times. He reached his little finger out to the rock, touched it—and there was a golden flash!

Quick, fast, Tippery ran about the field touching rocks with his little finger until all its magic had run out. Then Tippery and Patrick O'Michael looked at the rocks. But not a glitter of gold did they see. The rocks were still brown. Wait, there was one thing that glittered— Tippery's finger. Tippery's little finger had turned into gold! Oh, the disgrace! Tippery looked for a place to hide.

"Oh, begorra!" Patrick O'Michael wailed. "What good is a golden finger? I *would* catch the most forgetful leprechaun in all Ireland!"

And he gave one of the rocks a mighty whack with his dandelion shovel. But what was that? The rock split open, and it was white inside. Tippery poked it. He smelled it with his round nose. He licked it with his pointed tongue.

"We might try boiling it," he said.

Patrick and Tippery gathered up some of the hard, brown things and took them home. They put them in a pot of boiling water. When the things had cooked, Patrick and Tippery each took a bite, and the things were *good!*

"They may not be gold, but they're good to eat!" shouted Patrick O'Michael.

"Hooray!" cried the little man. "We put them in the *pot,* and we *ate* them. We'll call them potatoes!"

Then young Patrick and his leprechaun had fried potatoes for breakfast, and baked potatoes for dinner, and potato soup for supper. The next day they added dandelion greens to the potatoes and had potato salad. But they didn't eat all the potatoes. Tippery said they must save some to plant. Which they did.

When the new potatoes sprouted, they gave some to their neighbors, and then those neighbors gave some to other neighbors. Soon all Ireland had potatoes. But to this day, only the children's children of Patrick O'Michael O'Sullivan O'Callahan remember that they can thank a hungry leprechaun for potatoes.

# April Fool's Day

ARTHUR'S APRIL FOOL

MARC BROWN

It was the last day of March. The joke shop was full of people getting ready for April Fool's Day. Arthur and Buster tried out everything. Buster bought sneezing powder. Arthur got a fake telescope that gave whoever looked through it a black eye. But Arthur didn't feel like playing jokes. He kept thinking about Binky Barnes.

"Who is Binky Barnes?" asked Buster.

"Picture King Kong. Now double it," said Arthur. "He keeps threatening to punch me out."

The next day, Arthur was practicing his magic tricks with Buster and Francine for the April Fool's assembly.

"Hey, shrimp!" A giant shadow covered them. "I'll show *you* a trick," said Binky Barnes.

He grabbed Arthur's favorite pen and put it in his pocket.

"Now you see it, now you don't," said Binky.

"Hey, watch it," said Arthur, trying to look brave.

"Why don't you make me," said Binky, and walked away.

"Pick on someone your own size," called Francine. "Like Godzilla!"

"Wow," said Buster, "you were right. He's going to pulverize you!"

That night at dinner Arthur hardly ate anything. He didn't finish
his cheeseburger. He didn't even want any chocolate cream pie.

"What's the matter with Arthur?" asked his father.

"He's worried about getting pulverized," said D.W.

"Maybe he's been watching too many outer space movies," said his
mother.

Later on, D.W. barged into Arthur's room. "Good night, Mr. Uni-
verse," she said.

"Haven't you ever heard of knocking?" asked Arthur.

"After you get pulverized, can I have your room?" she asked.
"Beat it, D.W."

When Arthur finally fell asleep, he had nightmares. The next
morning, Francine offered Arthur a cookie.

"Yuk!" said Arthur. "This tastes like soap and toothpaste."

"April Fool!" laughed Francine.

But Arthur was too worried to laugh. "I'll never remember my
magic tricks for the assembly," he said.

"Calm down," said Buster. "I'll be your assistant. I'll help if you get
stuck."

32

Arthur felt better. He could count on Buster. But just before the assembly Buster got caught putting sneezing powder on Mr. Ratburn's desk. Instead of going to the assembly, Buster went to the principal's office.

"I'll blow it for sure without Buster," thought Arthur. He walked into the auditorium. Who was sitting in the front row? Binky Barnes. This was going to be even worse than he thought.

Arthur worried while Mr. Ratburn read people's minds. He worried while Francine and Muffy did shadow tricks. And he worried while the chorus sang "That Old Black Magic." Finally, it was his turn.

"For my first trick," said Arthur, "I'll need a volunteer . . ."

Binky Barnes jumped on the stage. "Surprise, pipsqueak!" he whispered.

Arthur gulped. Arthur asked Binky Barnes to tear up a sheet of paper and put it in the magic hat. He said the magic words and waved his magic wand to make the paper whole again. But rabbits came out instead.

Everyone laughed. Arthur took a bow. By mistake, flowers fell out of his sleeve. Binky Barnes laughed harder than anyone.

Then Arthur had an idea. He winked at Francine. "For my next trick I will saw this young man in half."

Binky stopped laughing and took a step back.

"My saw, please," said Arthur. Binky turned pale. "And now the bucket to collect the blood."

Binky screamed. He stepped back again, this time right off the stage. Everyone laughed, even Mr. Ratburn. After the assembly Arthur stopped Binky in the hall.

"What's the matter, Binky? You left before I could show you my best trick."

"No thanks," said Binky Barnes.

"Are you sure? It lets you see things you've never seen before," said Arthur.

"Really?" said Binky. He grabbed the telescope and pointed it at Francine. "I don't see anything."

"Of course not," said Arthur. "You have to know the secret words."

"Tell me!" said Binky.

"I can't," Arthur explained. "They're so secret I have to write them down—backwards. Do you have a pen?"

"Sure, here," said Binky. Arthur wrote the words. "Now go home, hold the paper up to the mirror, and you'll be able to read the secret words."

"Thanks, twerp," said Binky as he ran out the door.

"Boy, that's your best trick yet," said Buster. "You didn't get pulverized and you made Binky Barnes disappear."

"What did you write?" asked Francine.

# Passover

## The Magician

I. L. PERETZ

TRANSLATED BY MOSHE SPIEGEL AND

ADAPTED BY MARON L. WAXMAN

Once upon a time, just before Passover, a magician appeared in a small town in Poland. He was quite a sight. His clothes were all tattered and torn, and he wore a broken-down opera hat on his head. No one knew where he came from or where he was going, and if people asked him too many questions, he would disappear just like that—and then show up, a moment later, at the other end of town.

To show all his tricks, the magician rented a hall. And what tricks he did! He swallowed burning coals as if they were little dumplings, and he pulled ribbons—red, green, or any color you named—out of his mouth. One night he reached into his boots and out came one, two—no, sixteen—pairs of enormous gobbling turkeys. He could scrape gold coins off his worn-out soles, and when he whistled, rolls and breads flew into the hall, like birds. Then he whistled again, and they vanished.

But even though the magician could scrape coins off his shoes, he never seemed able to scrape together his rent. He could find turkeys and whistle for rolls, but he was always hungry. The man was a total mystery.

In the same village lived another poor, hungry man. Once the man had had a good lumber business, but he had lost it. The old lumberman hadn't worked for months, and he and his wife had sold everything they owned to get through the winter.

"How will we make the seder meal for Passover?" his wife asked as the holiday approached.

"I place my trust in God," the lumberman answered.

39

His wife searched the house from top to bottom, and in a dark, dusty corner she found an old silver spoon. "Sell this," she said, "and we can buy some matzos and wine for Passover."

At the market the lumberman sold the spoon, but on the way home he passed some wretched beggars. "Take these few coins," he said. "You're poorer than I am."

Passover came nearer, and the old couple still had no money to prepare for the holiday. "The Lord will not forget us," the old man reassured his wife.

At last Passover came. Every house in the village was spotless. Through the windows you could see the glow of candles, and silver sparkled on every table, polished for the wonderful holiday dinner when the story of Moses leading the Israelites out of slavery in Egypt is retold.

Only the old man's house was dark, but he stayed cheerful. "Happy holiday," he greeted his wife, kissing her gently.

"Happy holiday," she answered through her tears.

"Don't cry," the old man said. "The Lord must want us to sit at the table of one of our neighbors tonight. All doors are open on Passover. Come, take your shawl, and we'll find a friendly welcome."

Just then their door swung open. "Happy holiday," called a voice from the darkness. "May I be your guest tonight?"

"We would be happy to share with you," said the old man, "but we haven't any supper."

"I've brought supper with me," declared the voice.

And with that two pairs of silver candlesticks floated into the room and hung in the air. The old couple couldn't speak they were so astonished and afraid. Meanwhile, the magician busied himself with the rest of the seder preparations. He summoned the table to the center of the room and a snowy white cloth to spread over it. Now the candlesticks had a place to rest.

With a clap of his hand the magician called the rickety benches to the table and ordered them to get comfortable. Immediately they became soft chairs, covered with red velvet. White pillows appeared, too, so the guests could rest on them, the way you're supposed to at a seder. And then trays of food arrived—steaming soup, vegetables and meat, matzos, wine, and everything that is special for Passover.

Only when the table was all set did the old couple recover from their fright. "Is all this for us?" the old woman asked. "Are we allowed to eat it?"

"We must consult the rabbi," the old man said, and the two of them hurried off, leaving the magician standing at the table.

The rabbi listened to their story, then answered carefully. "Magic isn't real," he explained. "It fools only the eyes. If you can break the matzos and pour the wine and sit on the pillows, then your seder isn't magic. It's a gift from heaven, and you should enjoy it."

The old couple hurried home. The magician was gone, but before them lay the beautifully set table, with matzos that broke and wine that poured and fluffy pillows to sit on.

"The Lord has provided for us," the old man said, for just then he realized that the magical visitor who had come to their home was the prophet Elijah, the messenger of God. And so the old couple sat down to their seder with happy hearts.

# Easter

### PATIENCE

Chocolate Easter bunny
   In a jelly bean nest,
I'm saving you for very last
   Because I love you best.
I'll only take a nibble
   From the tip of your ear
And one bite from the other side
   So that you won't look queer.
Yum, you're so delicious!
   I didn't mean to eat
Your chocolate tail till Tuesday.
   Oops! There go your feet!
I wonder how your back tastes
   With all that chocolate hair.
I never thought your tummy
   Was only filled with air!
Chocolate Easter bunny
   In a jelly bean nest,
I'm saving you for very last
   Because I love you best.

BOBBI KATZ

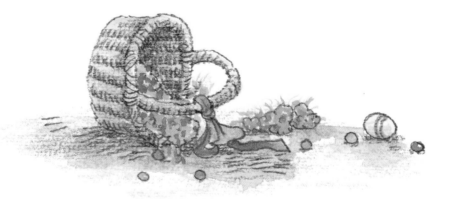

## THE EASTER PARADE

What shall I wear for the Easter Parade?
A dress that's the color of marmalade
With a border embroidered in light blue cornflowers
Like the edge of a meadow after spring showers
And a matching hat round as a top you can spin
And elastic to hold it on under my chin
And brand-new shoes whiter than newly poured cream
With heart-shaped, golden buckles that gleam;
And I'll carry a small purse of butterfly blue
With a penny for me and a penny for you
To buy us both glasses of cold lemonade
When we walk, hand in hand, in the Easter Parade.

WILLIAM JAY SMITH

## THE SUN ON EASTER DAY

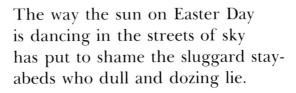

The way the sun on Easter Day
is dancing in the streets of sky
has put to shame the sluggard stay-
abeds who dull and dozing lie.

Get up! Get up! With harp and flute
make music fit to raise your roofs!
Grasses are leaping at the root.
Lambs are bounding on all four hoofs.

The very stones shake off their weight
and skip as seeds released from cold.
The soil itself, before too late,
blows up a storm of pollen gold.

All creatures, risen like the light,
in joyous motion join as one
to wish the winter gloom goodnight
and hail the dancing Easter sun.

NORMA FARBER

45

## A Lamb on the Table

CONCETTA C. DOUCETTE

Our family always had a lamb dinner on Easter Sunday. Lamb meat was my least favorite food, so I never thought about it, although I knew it was part of our Italian tradition. To me, lamb meant only that I would have to satisfy my hunger with bread and vegetables.

The only place we could buy lamb was downtown at the outdoor market. My father and I did the shopping together, and the minute we reached Hooper Street we could hear the salespeople competing with one another.

"Fresh lamb! Get your fresh lamb here!"

Papa asked a clerk for the youngest, fattest lamb. I wondered why the man was showing us live, penned animals.

Papa immediately pointed to a fat, woolly lamb. "Has it been fattened on grass and forage?"

"It has," the shopkeeper replied.

Papa asked its weight and the price. Numbers passed back and forth between them, but I didn't listen. I was so happy that my father was buying me a pet, and so busy feeling the curly fleece, I didn't hear what either of them said. It wasn't until Papa shook the man's hand and asked to have the lamb dressed, that my ears opened up. It was too good to be true. A lamb for a pet *and* an Easter outfit for it!

I pulled at my father's sleeve. "Oh, Papa, may I pick out the dress?"

"What dress?"

"The one for the lamb."

"What are you talking about?"

"You told the shopkeeper to dress the lamb, didn't you?"

"Yes, but—"

"Oh, Papa. Let me help him."

46

The shopkeeper had already lifted the lamb out of the pen. He looked at my father and shrugged.

Papa squatted down and put his hands on my shoulders. "I'm afraid you don't understand, Rosalie. Dressing an animal means butchering it."

I gasped. "Oh, Papa. You can't let him kill it."

"But, Rosalie, how else can we have lamb meat for Easter dinner?"

Tears rolled down my face. "How can you think of putting a piece of that beautiful lamb into your mouth?" I cried.

He didn't answer me.

"I'll tell Emilia and Angelo. They won't eat a bite of lamb Easter Sunday or ever again."

The shopkeeper became angry. He told my father that family arguments didn't cancel the deal. The handshake was binding. The lamb was ours. And he draped the lamb over my father's shoulders.

Papa knew that cooked lamb sitting in the icebox for days would go to waste. He was too wise and too thrifty to have food spoil. So Papa paid for the lamb and carried it across the back of his neck.

The trolley conductor tried to stop my father from carrying the lamb onto the car. But the tears on my face had not dried, and Papa had only to nod in my direction, and the man let us board. All the way home the lamb *baaed* because it was scared. It would have jumped off my father's shoulders if he had loosened his grip.

At home, Papa lifted the lamb over his head and set it down behind our iron fence. Our yard was small, but there was enough room for the animal to roam, and it liked being free.

Angelo and Emilia loved the surprise. Mama thought the lamb was cute, too, but she told us that if there was one complaint from our neighbors, it would have to go. The lamb had escaped its fate once. That's why we named it Close Call.

Close Call was a lovable and playful little ewe. All three of us wanted her to live and grow up and have lambs of her own. We knew Mama and Papa had talked about how long we could keep the lamb.

We also knew that Close Call was not just any animal to be butchered for meat. She was our pet, even though we'd only had her two days. I promised Emilia and Angelo that I would think of something special for Easter dinner—and find a place for Close Call to live.

We were discussing her when Papa called us. "It's time to bring our food baskets to church for Easter blessing," he said.

"What shall we do?" Emilia asked me. "We can't leave Close Call here alone. She'll get into Papa's rose bushes."

"We'll take her with us. The priest will understand." Angelo agreed, swung the lamb onto his shoulders, and headed for the church.

Emilia and I carried one basket between us. We peeked under the napkin. The basket held Mama's famous braided egg bread, anisette biscuits, and apple-butter cookies.

Papa asked us where Angelo was.

"He went ahead with Close Call," I told him.

At first Papa looked surprised. Then Mama gave him one of her special looks, and neither of them said anything. They picked up the other basket and carried it between them.

After blinking his eyes to make sure he wasn't seeing things, the priest blessed both Angelo and Close Call. He stroked the lamb's head and smiled sweetly. Mama held her head high as we left, and I knew she was proud to be with us.

It was much nicer going home than it had been going to church. Mama and Papa always left half the contents from each basket for the priests. Angelo was the only one who carried the same weight each way. Not only that, but some older boys made fun of him the entire time. Angelo walked so gaily, you'd think carrying a live lamb on his shoulders was the most natural thing in the world.

I thought and thought the rest of the afternoon and most of the night, too. Then I knew what I had to do.

Easter Sunday morning I went to first Mass. When I returned home I made coffee and set the breakfast table. After everyone else left for church, I felt very grown-up being alone in the house.

Mama had already brought up the fruits and vegetables she planned to serve for dinner. I opened the jars and prepared everything the way I had seen her do so many times before. Then I called my friend Connie, whose uncle was a farmer.

When the rest of the family arrived home from church, they noticed that I was carrying something fancy to the table. It was a woolly lamb made out of mashed potatoes.

I said, "I wanted you to have a lamb on the table. But I know Close Call is too frisky, and I didn't think it would be good to have her in the middle of our food."

Mama looked surprised, but she never said a word when I brought Close Call into the entryway. She understood that I wasn't finished with what I had to say.

Emilia, however, wanted to know how I had got Close Call dressed in one of my fancy toddler dresses and a bonnet.

I said, "I just told her how important it was, that's all."

Papa scratched his head. "I wouldn't believe it if I weren't seeing it."

I told Mama to read the note I had pinned to the ribbon around Close Call's neck.

She cried, but I knew it was because she was happy.

For weeks after that, Mama told anyone who would listen how lucky she was. "Not only did my Rosalie find a farmer to take the lamb for breeding, but she got us eggs and chickens for the rest of the year."

# Earth Day ✦ Arbor Day

## THINKING GREEN

If you look green, you're probably not feeling very well. But if the Earth is green, it's a healthy planet.

A green Earth means that plants are growing. It means that the soil is good, there's plenty of water, the air is clean, animals have places to live and things to eat.

And some wonderful news: Anyone can help keep the Earth green. It's so easy. You can plant a seed, give it some water, and watch it grow. You can save paper so that fewer trees will be cut down. You can "adopt" plants that are already growing and help them enjoy life.

Another important thing about plants (especially trees): They help fight the greenhouse effect and give us oxygen, which is the air we need to live.

What a deal!

We need lots of greenery in our world. Let's start planting!

THE EARTHWORKS GROUP

## BLOW-UP

Our cherry tree
Unfolds whole loads
Of pink-white bloom—
It just explodes.

For three short days
Its petals last.
Oh, what a waste.
But what a blast.

X. J. KENNEDY

## I'M GLAD

I'm glad the sky is painted blue
    And the earth is painted green,
With such a lot of nice fresh air
    All sandwiched in between.

ANONYMOUS

## TREES

The trees share their shade with
    all who pass by,
But their leaves whisper secrets
    only to the wind.

NELDA DISHMAN

53

# Mother's Day

MOTHER, MOTHER, I WANT ANOTHER

MARIA POLUSHKIN ROBBINS

It was bedtime in the mouse house. Mrs. Mouse took baby mouse to his room. She helped him put on his pajamas and told him to brush his teeth.

She tucked him into his bed and read him a bedtime story. She gave him a bedtime kiss, and then she said, "Good night."

But as she was leaving, baby mouse started to cry.

"Why are you crying?" asked Mrs. Mouse.

"I want another, Mother."

"Another mother!" cried Mrs. Mouse. "Where will I find another mother for my baby?"

Mrs. Mouse ran to get Mrs. Duck. "Please, Mrs. Duck, come to our house and help put baby mouse to bed. Tonight he wants another mother."

Mrs. Duck came and sang a song:

*Quack, quack, mousie,*
*Don't you fret.*
*I'll bring you worms*
*Both fat and wet.*

But baby mouse said, "Mother, Mother, I want another."

Mrs. Duck went to get Mrs. Frog. Mrs. Frog came and sang:

*Croak, croak, mousie,*
*Close your eyes.*
*I will bring you*
*Big fat flies.*

But baby mouse said, "Mother, Mother, I want another."

Mrs. Frog went to get Mrs. Pig. Mrs. Pig came and sang a song:

> *Oink, oink, mousie,*
> *Go to sleep.*
> *I'll bring some carrots*
> *For you to keep.*

But baby mouse said, "Mother, Mother, I want another."

Mrs. Pig went to get Mrs. Donkey. Mrs. Donkey came and sang a song:

> *Hee-haw, mousie,*
> *Hush-a-bye.*
> *I'll sing for you*
> *A lullaby.*

But baby mouse had had enough. "NO MORE MOTHERS!" he shouted. "I want another KISS."

"Well, now!" said Mrs. Duck.

"Really?" said Mrs. Frog.

"Indeed?" said Mrs. Pig.

"I see," said Mrs. Donkey.

Mrs. Duck kissed baby mouse. Mrs. Frog kissed baby mouse. Mrs. Pig kissed baby mouse. And Mrs. Donkey kissed baby mouse. Then Mrs. Mouse gave baby mouse a drink of water. She tucked in his blanket, and she gave him a kiss.

Baby mouse smiled. "May I have another, Mother?"

"Of course," said Mrs. Mouse, and she leaned over and gave him *another* kiss.

# Memorial Day

### WHEN JOHNNY COMES MARCHING HOME AGAIN

When Johnny comes marching home again, hurrah! hurrah!
We'll give him a hearty welcome then, hurrah! hurrah!
The men will cheer and the boys will shout,
The ladies they will all turn out,
And we'll all feel joy when Johnny comes marching home.

The old church bell will peal with joy, hurrah! hurrah!
To welcome home our darling boy, hurrah! hurrah!
The village lads and lassies say with roses they will strew the way,
And we'll all feel joy when Johnny comes marching home.

**FOLKSONG**

# Happy Birthday

### IF WE DIDN'T HAVE BIRTHDAYS

If we didn't have birthdays, you wouldn't be you.
If you'd never been born, well then what would you do?
If you'd never been born, well then what would you be?
You *might* be a fish! Or a toad in a tree!
You might be a doorknob! Or three baked potatoes!
You might be a bag full of hard green tomatoes.
Or worse than all that . . . Why, you might be a WASN'T!
A Wasn't has no fun at all. No, he doesn't.
A Wasn't just isn't. He just isn't present.
But you . . . You ARE YOU! And, now isn't that pleasant!

DR. SEUSS

### THE END

When I was One,
I had just begun.

When I was Two,
I was nearly new.

When I was Three,
I was hardly Me.

When I was Four,
I was not much more.

When I was Five,
I was just alive.

But now I am Six, I'm as clever as clever,
So I think I'll be six now for ever and ever.

A. A. MILNE

## GOOD-BYE, SIX—HELLO, SEVEN

I'm getting a higher bunk bed.
And I'm getting a bigger bike.
And I'm getting to cross Connecticut Avenue
    all by myself, if I like.
And I'm getting to help do dishes.
And I'm getting to weed the yard.
And I'm getting to think that seven
    could be hard.

JUDITH VIORST

## FOR SOMEONE ON HIS TENTH BIRTHDAY

So you're ten! Why that's *two* numbers old!
(As I hope you know without being told.)
It takes a One and a Zero, too,
To count up someone as old as you.
Just think how many years it has been
Since you started your one-number years. All ten!
(That's a lot to think back to, sir.) And then,
Think how many years it will be
Before you change from two numbers to three!

That's why I have it in mind to say
That TEN is the hugest-of-all birthday,
And maybe the gayest, and maybe the best.
It does change more numbers than all the rest
For at least another ninety years!
(That's something to think about!) So here's
To someone TEN! And here's three cheers
For a boy who has changed from one number to two,
And here's my wish (and may it come true):
May you learn to like soap (here's a sample cake free)
By the time you change from two numbers to three!

JOHN CIARDI

61

# Father's Day

## A DAY WHEN FROGS WEAR SHOES

ANN CAMERON

My little brother, Huey, my best friend, Gloria, and I were sitting on our front steps. It was one of those hot summer days when everything stands still. We didn't know what to do. We were watching the grass grow. It didn't grow fast.

"You know something?" Gloria said. "This is a slow day."

"It's so slow the dogs don't bark," Huey said.

"It's so slow the flies don't fly," Gloria said.

"It's so slow ice cream wouldn't melt," I said.

"If we had any ice cream," Huey said.

"But we don't," Gloria said.

We watched the grass some more.

"We better do something," I said.

"Like what?" Gloria asked.

"We could go visit Dad," Huey said.

"That's a *terrible* idea," I said.

"Why?" Huey asked. "I like visiting Dad."

My father has a shop about a mile from our house, where he fixes cars. Usually it is fun to visit him. If he has customers, he always introduces us as if we were important guests. If he doesn't have company, sometimes he lets us ride in the cars he puts up on the lift. Sometimes he buys us treats.

"Huey," I said, "usually, visiting Dad is a good idea. Today, it's a dangerous idea."

"Why?" Gloria said.

"Because we're bored," I said. "My dad hates it when people are bored. He says the world is so interesting nobody should ever be bored."

"I see," Gloria said, as if she didn't.

"So we'll go see him," Huey said, "and we just won't tell him we're bored. We're bored, but we won't tell him."

"Just so you remember that!" I said.

"Oh, I'll remember," Huey said.

Huey was wearing his angel look. When he has that look, you know he'll never remember anything.

The sun shined up at us from the sidewalks. Even the shadows on the street were hot as blankets.

Huey picked up a stick and scratched it along the sidewalk.

"Oh, we're bored," he muttered. "Bored, bored, bored, bored, bored."

"Huey!" I yelled. I wasn't bored any more. I was nervous.

Finally we reached a sign:

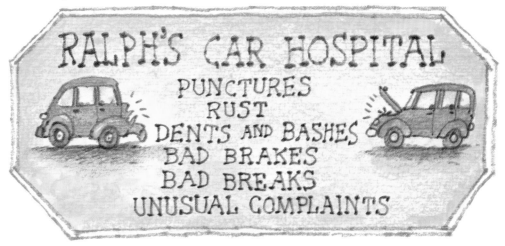

RALPH'S CAR HOSPITAL
PUNCTURES
RUST
DENTS AND BASHES
BAD BRAKES
BAD BREAKS
UNUSUAL COMPLAINTS

That's my dad's sign. My dad is Ralph.

The parking lot had three cars in it. Dad was inside the shop, lifting the hood of another car.

"Hi, Dad," I said.

"Hi!" my dad said.

"We're—" Huey said.

I didn't trust Huey. I stepped on his foot.

"We're on a hike," I said.

"Well, nice of you to stop by," my father said. "If you want, you can stay awhile and help me."

"O.K.," we said.

So Huey sorted nuts and bolts. Gloria shined fenders with a rag. I held a new windshield wiper while my dad put it on a car window.

"Nice work, Huey and Julian and Gloria!" my dad said when we were done.

And then he sent us to the store across the street to buy paper cups and ice cubes and a can of frozen lemonade.

We mixed the lemonade in the shop. Then we sat out under the one tree by the side of the driveway and drank all of it.

"Good lemonade!" my father said. "So what are you kids going to do now?"

"Oh, hike!" I said.

"You know," my father answered, "I'm surprised at you kids picking a hot day like today for a hike. The ground is so hot. On a day like this, frogs wear shoes!"

"They do?" Huey said.

"Especially if they go hiking," my father said. "Of course, a lot of frogs, on a day like this, would stay home. So I wonder why you kids are hiking."

Sometimes my father notices too much. Then he gets yellow lights shining in his eyes, asking you to tell the whole truth. That's when I know to look at my feet.

"Oh," I said, "we *like* hiking."

But Gloria didn't know any better. She looked into my father's eyes. "Really," she said, "this wasn't a real hike. We came to see you."

"Oh, I see!" my father said, looking pleased.

"Because we were bored," Huey said.

My father jumped up so fast he tipped over his lemonade cup. "BORED!" my father yelled. "You were BORED?"

He picked up his cup and waved it in the air.

"And you think *I* don't get BORED?" my father roared, sprinkling out a few last drops of lemonade from his cup. "You think I don't get bored fixing cars when it's hot enough that frogs wear shoes?"

" 'This is such an interesting world that nobody should ever be bored.' That's what you said," I reminded him.

"Last week," Huey added.

"Ummm," my father said. He got quiet.

He rubbed his hand over his mouth, the way he does when he's thinking.

"Why, of course," my father said, "I remember that. And it's the perfect, absolute truth. People absolutely SHOULD NOT get bored! However—" He paused. "It just happens that, sometimes, they do."

"You know, if you three would kindly help me some more, I could leave a half hour early, and we could drive down by the river."

"We'll help," I said.

"Yes, and then we can look for frogs!" Huey said. So we stayed. We learned how to make a signal light blink. And afterward, on the way to the river, my dad bought us all ice cream cones. The ice cream did melt. Huey's melted all down the front of his shirt. It took him ten paper napkins and the river to clean up. After Huey's shirt was clean, we took our shoes and socks off and went wading.

We looked for special rocks under the water—the ones that are beautiful until you take them out of the water, when they get dry and not so bright.

We found skipping stones and tried to see who could get the most skips from a stone.

We saw a school of minnows going as fast as they could to get away from us.

But we didn't see any frogs.

"If you want to see frogs," my father said, "you'll have to walk down the bank a ways and look hard."

So we decided to do that.

"Fine!" my father said. "But I'll stay here. I think I'm ready for a little nap."

"Naps are boring!" we said.

"Sometimes it's nice to be bored," my father said.

We left him with his eyes closed, sitting under a tree.

Huey saw the first frog. He almost stepped on it. It jumped into the water, and we ran after it.

Huey caught it and picked it up, and then I saw another one. I grabbed it. It was slippery and strong, and its body was cold, just like it wasn't the middle of the summer. Then Gloria caught one too. The frogs wriggled in our hands, and we felt their hearts beating. Huey looked at their funny webbed feet.

"Their feet are good for swimming," he said, "but Dad is wrong. They don't wear shoes!"

"No way," Gloria said.

"Let's go tell him," I said.

We threw our frogs back into the river. They made little trails swimming away from us. And then we went back to my father.

He was sitting under the tree with his eyes shut. It looked like he hadn't moved an inch.

"We found frogs," Huey said, "and we've got news for you. They don't wear shoes!"

My father's eyes opened. "They don't?" he said. "Well, I can't be right about everything. Dry your feet. Put your shoes on. It's time to go."

68

We all sat down to put on our shoes.

I pulled out a sock and put it on.

I stuck my foot into my shoe. My foot wouldn't go in.

I picked up the shoe and looked inside.

"Oh no!" I yelled.

There were two little eyes inside my shoe, looking out at me. Huey and Gloria grabbed their socks. All our shoes had frogs in them, every one.

"What did I tell you," my father said.

"You were right," we said. "It's a day when frogs wear shoes!"

# Summer Vacation

## SCHOOL IS ALL OVER

School is all over,
I'm in the next grade—
And it's picnics and popsicles,
Pink lemonade,
Sunburns and sailing
And feet that are bare,
T-shirts and sneakers
And sand in my hair,
Swimming and rowing
And fisherman's fun.
It's hard to believe it,
But summer's begun.

**ALICE LOW**

## THE LITTLE JUMPING GIRLS

Jump—jump—jump—
   Jump over the moon;
Jump all the morning
   And all the noon.

Jump—jump—jump—
   Jump all night;
Won't our mothers
   Be in a fright?

Jump—jump—jump—
   Over the sea;
What wonderful wonders
   We shall see.

Jump—jump—jump—
   Jump far away;
And all come home
   Some other day.

**KATE GREENAWAY**

## WHAT SHALL I PACK IN THE BOX MARKED "SUMMER"?

A handful of wind that I caught with a kite
A firefly's flame in the dark of the night
The green grass of June that I tasted with toes
The flowers I knew from the tip of my nose
The clink of the ice cubes in pink lemonade
The fourth of July Independence parade!
The sizzle of hot dogs, the fizzle of coke
Some pickles and mustard and barbecue smoke
The print of my fist in the palm of my mitt,
As I watched for the batter to strike out or hit
The splash of the water, the top-to-toe cool
Of a stretch-and-kick trip through a blue swimming pool
The tangle of night songs that slipped through my screen
Of crickets and insects too small to be seen
The seed pods that formed on the flowers to say
That summer was packing her treasures away.

BOBBI KATZ

### VACATION

In my head I hear a humming
*Summer summer summer's coming.*
Soon we're going on vacation,
But there is a complication.
Day by day the problem's growing
We don't know yet where we're going!

    Mother likes the country best,
    That's so she can read and rest.
    Dad thinks resting is a bore,
    He's for fishing at the shore.
    Sailing is my brother's pick,
    Sailing makes my sister sick.
    She says swimming's much more cool,
    Swimming in a swimming pool.
    As for me, why, I don't care
    I'd be happy anywhere

In my head I hear a humming
*Summer summer summer's coming.*
Soon we're going on vacation,
But we have a complication.
Day by day the problem's growing
Where oh where will we be going?

MARY ANN HOBERMAN

SEA SHELL

Sea Shell, Sea Shell,
  Sing me a song, O please!
A song of ships, and sailormen,
  And parrots, and tropical trees,

Of islands lost in the Spanish Main
Which no man ever may find again,
Of fishes and corals under the waves,
And sea horses stabled in great green caves.

Sea Shell, Sea Shell,
Sing of the things you know so well.

AMY LOWELL

IF ONCE YOU HAVE SLEPT ON AN ISLAND

If once you have slept on an island
  You'll never be quite the same;
You may look as you looked the day before
  And go by the same old name,

You may bustle about in street and shop;
  You may sit at home and sew,
But you'll see blue water and wheeling gulls
  Wherever your feet may go.

You may chat with the neighbors of this and that
  And close to your fire keep,
But you'll hear ship whistle and lighthouse bell
  And tides beat through your sleep.

Oh, you won't know why, and you can't say how
  Such change upon you came,
But—once you have slept on an island
  You'll never be quite the same!

RACHEL FIELD

#  Canada Day

### FIREWORKS

Pin wheels whirling round
Spit sparks upon the ground,
And rockets shoot up high
And blossom in the sky—
Blue and yellow, green and red
Flowers falling on my head,
And I don't ever have to go
To bed, to bed, to bed!

DOROTHY ALDIS

## AND MY HEART SOARS

The beauty of the trees,
the softness of the air,
the fragrance of the grass,
   speaks to me.

The summit of the mountain,
the thunder of the sky,
the rhythm of the sea,
   speaks to me.

The faintness of the stars,
the freshness of the morning,
the dew drop on the flower,
   speaks to me.

The strength of fire,
the taste of salmon,
the trail of the sun,
And the life that never goes away,
   They speak to me.

And my heart soars.

**CHIEF DAN GEORGE**

# Independence Day

## Caddie's Independence Day

CAROL RYRIE BRINK

The Woodlawn girls were all getting new white dresses for the Independence Day celebration at Eau Galle.

"It really seems a waste of good material to make one for Caddie," said Mother, with a sigh. "She's ruined every white dress we ever made for her."

"But she's doing so much better now, Mother," said Caddie's sister Clara gently.

Just then Caddie and her friend Katie came in, right on time for a fitting. Caddie slipped out of her old blue denim and into the yards of white muslin.

Caddie regarded herself in the mirror.

"Is that me?" she said. "My goodness! I won't know how to act out of blue denim."

"You act like a lady, that's what you do," advised Mother. "You take small steps and turn out your toes when you walk, and keep away from horses and the snags on rail fences, and don't sit on the grass or climb the haymow or eat strawberries or write with ink."

"I might as well be dead," said Caddie, screwing up her nose. "Is a white dress worth it?"

"Oh, yes," said Katie. "You look lovely, Caddie. Honest, you do."

There never was such a celebration as they had at Eau Galle that year. The celebration centered about the mill. The loading platform at the back was turned for the day into a speaker's rostrum and hung with flags and bunting, while the open ground beyond was reserved for people to sit with their campstools and their picnic baskets. The millpond was to be the scene of various water sports. There was a place for land sports, too, and a poplar tree, stripped of its bark and branches and greased to make climbing difficult, had already been set up with a ham tied to the top as a prize for the first man or boy who should successfully climb it. And in the evening there were to be fireworks.

Caddie cast a regretful glance at the pole. *Well, that was no place for a white dress, at any rate,* she thought.

Catching the greased pig would not be proper sport for her either, she decided regretfully. Mother never contrived fine clothes for the boys on the Fourth of July, because they were expected to get into everything; but the girls were dressed up like china dolls and expected to stay sweet and spotless.

"Oh, well," Caddie told herself, "I *will* be clean and ladylike this year, no matter what. I'll just surprise them all for once."

To celebrate the Fourth of July meant something definite in those days. The Civil War was still close enough, and even the War of the Revolution, to make them thankful for peace and liberty. It was a kind of summer Thanksgiving Day when they could raise their voices in gratitude for life, liberty, and the pursuit of happiness, and dedicate themselves anew to the self-evident truth that all men are created equal.

Father's voice, full of the fervor of the day, started them all to singing "The Battle Hymn of the Republic," and Caddie's heart swelled as she sang.

She kept humming part of it to herself as she wandered about the picnic ground.

> Oh, be swift, my soul, to answer Him!
>     Be jubilant, my feet!
> Our God is marching on

Caddie and Katie were early enough to greet the other girls as they arrived in their white dresses with red, white, and blue bunting looped over the shoulder and knotted at the waist. All the girls were to sit on the loading platform behind the speakers, and sing before and after the speeches were delivered. But until the speaking began, they were free to roam about as they wished.

Tom and Warren with a crowd of boys went past them toward the millpond, and Tom called back over his shoulder, "They're starting to roll logs. You better come watch."

"Let's do," said Caddie to Katie, and Katie said, "All right."

"Just look out for your dress, that's all," warned Clara. "Mother will be wild if she sees you standing up to sing and the front of your dress all torn."

"Oh, bother!" Caddie said. "They're always plaguing me about my clothes. But nothing—*nothing's* going to happen to this one!"

In the millpond floated several large peeled logs, and lumber-jacks from the various logging camps up the river were trying their skill upon them. From a boat each man would carefully mount his log, and balance himself on it while he rolled it under his feet. Much skill was required to stay on the slippery logs at all, and sooner or later one of the men would lose his balance, slip off, and go down with a great splash.

The children soon had their favorites among the contestants, and cheered or shouted praise or disapproval. When Robert Ireton came out in old blue jeans with his strong brown arms folded across his bare chest, waiting for someone to row him to a log, the Woodlawn children and all the children of their neighborhood went mad with glee.

*"Robert! Robert!"* They shouted. "We're on your side, Robert! Beat the lumber camps, Robert! Show 'em Dunnville's got the champion log roller of the world!"

Little Ezra McCantry came to stand in front of Caddie and Katie so he could see better, and Caddie saw Ezra's toe go out experimentally to one of the floating logs.

"I c'n walk 'em, too," he said, "as good as Robert Ireton."

"Well, don't you try it, mister," Caddie advised.

Now Robert had reached his log and mounted it. His feet were light and quick on the rolling log. He might have been dancing one of his Irish jigs on the threshing floor of the barn at home, to see him lift his feet. He was better, more light and graceful, than the lumbermen from up the river.

But suddenly, in the midst of her pleasure and excitement at Robert's success, Caddie saw out of the corner of her eye that another log walker was performing near at hand. Ezra McCantry was stepping gingerly from log to log, and running the length of them and back with arms outstretched to keep his balance.

"Come back here, Ezra!" Caddie cried.

But Ezra only ran a little farther out and called back mockingly, "Look at me! Look at me! I c'n walk 'em, too!"

Even as he uttered his howl of triumph, the log he was on began to roll. Slowly and gently it rolled, but it took Ezra by surprise and he rolled with it. He made a wonderful, big splash for such a very small boy.

"*Oh, dear!*" cried Caddie. "*Oh, dear!*"—and all sorts of discon-nected things went like a panic through her mind. "*Be swift, my soul. Be jubilant, my feet. . . .* But, oh, my dress! Whatever happens, it must not get wet."

And then she saw Ezra coming up to the surface and clawing the air an instant, trying to catch the log—and going down again without having succeeded. She knew that the millpond was deep, and that Ezra couldn't swim—and neither could she. She heard people be-hind her beginning to shout, and Katie bursting into tears. Then, before she knew it, her clean white slippers were stepping out on the first logs and then the next ones, and she was frantically untying the long piece of bunting which had been over her shoulder.

She heard her own vice calling, "*Ezra! Ezra!*"

When he came up again she was still calling, and somehow she got his attention and flung one end of the bunting near enough to his clutching hands so that he could grasp it.

As he went down again, clutching the bunting, it snapped out tight, like a kite string in the wind, and Caddie, holding the other end, felt the log she was on beginning to roll. She tried to make her feet go fast, like Robert's feet, in order to keep her balance; but still her log kept rolling, rolling—and the clean white slippers with the satin rosettes could not go fast enough. There was a second wonderful splash—and it was Caddie Woodlawn!

But she never let go of the bunting; and Ezra was holding on to his end, too. There was a log between them, and with the bunting over it neither one of them could go down too far. Caddie struggled desperately up until she could cling to the log with one hand and pull in the bunting with the other; and presently Ezra was clinging to the other side of the log, coughing and blowing water. With one on each side of it the log had stopped rolling, and they could hold to it and catch their breath for a moment until help came.

Robert was the first to reach them, swimming from his log in mid-pond with long, sure strokes.

"Oh, Robert!" Caddie cried, between gulps and coughs. "You had to get off your log! We made you lose the contest, Robert."

"Eh, divil take the contest," Robert roared, "and my Caddie drowning! What do you think, lass? What do you think!"

When they were safe on shore again, with the water running from them in streams and an anxious crowd surging around them, Caddie looked down and saw that she was still clutching the Fourth of July bunting against her breast. The red and blue dye was running in gaudy little streams all down the front of her lovely new white dress. As she stood there speechless with this new calamity which topped all the others, she heard the first notes of the fife and drum calling the people to the speaking and the singing.

"Oh, come along now, Caddie," Katie said, "You'll dry out on the speakers' stand, with all the hot sun blazing in there. It's time we went to sing."

"But I can't! I can't—*like this*," wailed Caddie.

Tom and Katie, Warren and Hetty and little Minnie were all around her, helping her wring out the yards of white—and *blue* and *red* muslin.

"Sure you can, Caddie," they were saying. "They need your high voice on the choruses."

"You can sit in the back," said Katie, "and I'll spread my skirts out over yours."

"But Mother!" gasped Caddie. "She'll take one look at me and have a heart attack."

"Just come along," they said.

Caddie and Katie had just time to squeeze in among the other girls at the back of the platform before the program began. Caddie was sure that Mother could not have seen the dreadful mess she was wearing.

When the fifes and drums were silent, the girls' chorus stood up and began to sing. Caddie remained seated so that she would not spoil the beautiful appearance of the other girls, but her voice soared clear and happy.

It seemed as if half of the men of Dunnville and Eau Galle made speeches that day; but Dr. Nightingale made the last one, and it was the best one too. He spoke very simply, as if he were talking to friends—as, indeed, he was. He said that the truest way citizens could serve their country was by obeying its laws and by meeting daily life with courage and honesty. Good citizens, he said, were worth more to a nation than good soldiers or good policemen.

He said, "There are many good citizens among us, but it has just been called to my attention that one of us today has proven particularly worthy of citizenship. This person, although one of the youngest members of our society, has proven equal to an emergency which called for quick thinking, courage, and a willingness to risk personal safety. You all know this young person; you have just heard her voice in the singing. When you know that Caddie Woodlawn saved a little boy's life this morning, I think you will want her to step forward and receive your cheers."

Until her name was mentioned, Caddie had been looking around trying to imagine whom Dr. Nightingale was speaking of. Now when she heard him saying "Will Caddie Woodlawn please come forward?" Caddie was so filled with astonishment and alarm that she could do nothing but sit there and whisper, "Oh, I can't!"

"Don't be silly," the girls cried, pushing her forward.

To her surprise Caddie found herself going up to the front of the platform where Dr. Nightingale stood with outstretched hand and welcoming smile. Caddie had tried to hold the worst parts of her bedraggled skirt together so that it would not show, but when she held out her hand it all fell open so that everyone could see that Caddie Woodlawn had spoiled another white dress.

Dr. Nightingale seemed to understand her distress just as he understood measles or mumps.

"Congratulations, Caddie," he said, "and don't be ashamed of your dress, my dear. I'm proud to shake the hand of a girl who can forget her vanity to risk her life for others."

Caddie looked up at him in pleased surprise, and then down to the blur of faces below her; and suddenly two faces stood out clearly. Mother and Father were sitting side by side, and both of their faces were full of pride and happiness.

Well, it was a lovely day—a day to remember all one's life!

Caddie did not roll logs or chase the greased pig, nor climb the greased pole; but even in her bedraggled dress she had a lovely time. She saw Tom scale the slippery pole and win the ham and Robert Ireton outlast the men from the lumber camps and win the five-dollar gold piece for staying longest on his log. For everyone had agreed that he should not be disqualified from entering the final contest because he had jumped off his log in the morning to go to the assistance of Caddie and Ezra.

In the evening they all rode home on the hayload, tired but content, and as they rode they sang. An early moon was in the sky, and the odors of sweet clover and red clover and new-cut hay and pine mingled like perfume in the clear air. And, when their songs had drifted away again to silence, Caddie found herself softly humming the other tune which seemed so perfectly to fit the day, and the new, sweet country which they loved so well.

Oh, be swift, my soul, to answer him!
Be jubilant, my feet!

# Friendship Day

## NEIGHBORS

The Cobbles live in the house next door,
In the house with the prickly pine.
Whenever I see them, they ask, "How are you?"
And I always answer, "I'm fine."
And I always ask them, "Is Jonathan home?"
(Jonathan Cobble is nine.)
I'm Jonathan Cobble's very best friend
And Jonathan Cobble is mine.

MARY ANN HOBERMAN

## SINCE HANNA MOVED AWAY

The tires on my bike are flat.
The sky is grouchy gray.
At least it sure feels like that
Since Hanna moved away.

Chocolate ice cream tastes like prunes.
December's come to stay.
They've taken back the Mays and Junes
Since Hanna moved away.

Flowers smell like halibut.
Velvet feels like hay.
Every handsome dog's a mutt
Since Hanna moved away.

Nothing's fun to laugh about.
Nothing's fun to play.
They call me, but I won't come out
Since Hanna moved away.

JUDITH VIORST

## THE OPPOSITE OF TWO

What is the opposite of *two*?
*A lonely me, a lonely you.*

RICHARD WILBUR

# Labor Day

TEDDY GETS A JOB

JOHANNA HURWITZ

Mommy was helping Nora pack a small suitcase. She was going to have a sleep-over visit with her friend Sharon for *two* nights. It was the first time that she would be away for so long. Teddy watched her with admiration. He wished that he was as grown up as Nora, but he didn't want to have to sleep in another house for two nights to prove it. Now that he was in kindergarten, everyone said he was a big boy. But whatever he did, Nora had already done it before. He wished that just once he could do something that Nora had never done.

Nora was deciding whether she should pack her red polo shirt with blue stripes or her blue polo shirt with red stripes when the doorbell rang. Nora threw both shirts on her bed and ran with her mother to open the door. Teddy followed behind. It was always interesting when the doorbell rang.

At the door stood their across-the-hall neighbor, Anita. "Hi!" she greeted them all. "I've come to ask a favor. Actually, I want to offer Nora a job."

"A job? A job for me? Will I get money?" asked Nora with delight.

"Of course you'll get paid, if your mother agrees," said Anita. "Because of the holiday weekend, I'm going to be away tomorrow night. And I wondered if you would be able to feed Cassandra and give her fresh water while I'm gone."

"Oh, yes!" shouted Nora. Cassandra was the large, white cat that Anita had acquired a few months before.

"Nora, you won't be home," Mommy reminded her. "You will be at Sharon's all weekend."

"Oh, no!" said Nora, stamping her foot with anger. Two minutes ago she had been happy about going to Sharon's, and now she was sorry.

"That's too bad," said Anita. "I guess I'll ask Eugene Spencer if he would like the job." Eugene had recently moved to the fourth floor, and he was eight years old.

"Eugene Spencer has a sore throat and a temperature," said Nora.

"I could do it," offered Teddy.

"What a good idea!" said Anita. "Cassandra knows and trusts you. All you have to do is open a fresh can of cat food tomorrow morning."

"You can't work can openers, Teddy," said Nora.

Teddy thought for a minute. "You could open the can and leave it inside the refrigerator," he said to Anita. "I can open a refrigerator."

"How will you get inside the apartment?" asked Nora.

"Oh, I'll leave my key, of course," said Anita.

"You don't know how to open doors with keys," Nora reminded Teddy.

"I'll open the door for him," said their mother, "as long as I don't have to go inside." Mommy was allergic to cats. They made her eyes get red and tear, and they made her sneeze, too.

So it was arranged, and Teddy had a job. He could hardly wait to give Cassandra her meal. He wanted to go the minute that he woke up in the morning, but Mommy said that first he had to eat his own breakfast and that he had to put his clothes on, too.

"Cassandra is hungry," said Teddy. But he quickly dressed and, as usual, put on his Superman cape.

Mommy opened Anita's door for Teddy. He went inside. Cassandra had heard the sound of the key in the lock, and she stood in the hallway rubbing herself against Teddy's legs. He closed the door behind him and went into the kitchen.

It felt strange to be in Anita's apartment without Anita. Teddy was glad that he was wearing his cape. It made him feel strong and brave, even if there wasn't anything to be afraid of. Teddy stood on tiptoe and turned on the kitchen-light switch. He felt better now that there was more light.

Cassandra kept meowing, so Teddy hurried to open the refrigerator. Sure enough, right in front was the can of cat food waiting to be served. Teddy put the can on the floor for Cassandra and picked up her water bowl. It was almost empty. Since he couldn't reach the faucets at the sink, he pushed a chair over and climbed up on it.

He filled the bowl with cold water and climbed down. As he did so, he tipped the bowl and water spilled all over the floor. Teddy looked for something he could use to wipe it up. There was a paper-towel roller, but there were no towels on it. He looked in the sink for a sponge. There was nothing. It wouldn't be nice to leave puddles of water on the floor, thought Teddy. He wiped his wet hands on his cape and then decided that he should take it off and use it as a towel. Cassandra didn't pay any attention to Teddy as he mopped up the water. She was too busy eating her tuna fish.

Then Teddy noticed for the first time that there was a faint buzzing sound in the apartment. It had a steady ring, and it just kept on and on. It wasn't the doorbell. Teddy knew what that sounded like. It wasn't the telephone. Teddy listened hard, trying to figure out what the sound was. Maybe there was a burglar in Anita's bedroom, and he was ringing a bell to make Teddy go away. Teddy began to feel afraid. He was going to rush back to the safety of his own apartment when a thought occurred to him. Maybe the burglar would kidnap Cassandra. Quietly, so the burglar wouldn't hear him, Teddy walked toward the direction of the ringing, which was coming from Anita's bedroom. Teddy pushed the door open. The room was rather dark and he couldn't see too well, but the ringing was much louder.

"You can't steal Cassandra," he shouted into the room.

There was no answer.

He walked inside the room and turned on the light. There on the table by Anita's bed was her alarm clock, and it was ringing. Anita must have forgotten and put the switch on. Teddy went over to the clock and figured out how to turn off the sound. Then he turned off the light in the bedroom and returned to the kitchen.

"It's all right, Cassandra. You're safe," he reassured the cat. She didn't seem worried at all. She just went on eating.

Teddy finished mopping up the water and refilled the cat's water bowl again. This time he managed to put it on the floor without spilling it.

"Good-bye Cassandra. Don't be lonely. Anita will be back tomorrow," said Teddy. He was glad that his mother didn't give him food just once a day.

He took his wet cape and returned to his own apartment. "It's a good thing that I had this with me," he told his mother. "It came in very handy. Superman only uses his cape for flying, but I had to use mine for drying. There weren't any towels in Anita's kitchen, so I used my cape instead."

"Good thinking!" said Teddy's mother. She put the cape into the laundry hamper, and Teddy went downstairs to the second floor to play with Russell.

When Anita returned home that evening, she rang the doorbell and presented Teddy with a dollar bill.

"You did a fine job taking care of Cassandra," she told Teddy. "You are a super cat-sitter."

"What are you going to do with your money?" Nora asked.

"I'll put it in my bank and save it," he said. He was proud of his dollar bill, but he was even prouder of something else. He had earned money, and Nora had never done that. For the first time Teddy had done something first, before Nora. That made having a job even more special.

# First Day of School

SUMMER GOES

Summer goes, summer goes
Like the sand between my toes
When the waves go out.
That's how summer pulls away,
Leaves me standing here today,
Waiting for the school bus.

Summer brought, summer brought
All the frogs that I have caught,
Frogging at the pond,
Hot dogs, flowers, shells and rocks,
Postcards in my postcard box—
Places far away.

Summer took, summer took
All the lessons in my book,
Blew them far away.
I forgot the things I knew—
Arithmetic and spelling too,
Never thought about them.

Summer's gone, summer's gone—
Fall and winter coming on,
Frosty in the morning.
Here's the school bus right on time.
I'm not really sad that I'm
Going back to school.

RUSSELL HOBAN

BEVERLY CLEARY

"Ha-ha, I get to ride the bus to school all by myself," Ramona bragged to her big sister, Beatrice, at breakfast. Her stomach felt quivery with excitement at the day ahead, a day that would begin with a bus ride just the right length to make her feel a long way from home but not long enough—she hoped—to make her feel carsick.

"Ha-ha yourself." Beezus was too excited to be annoyed with her little sister. "Today I start high school."

"*Junior* high school," corrected Ramona, who was not going to let her sister get away with acting older than she really was. "Rosemont Junior High School is not the same as high school, and besides you have to walk."

After the family's rush to brush teeth, Mr. Quimby said to his daughters, "Hold out your hands," and into each waiting pair he dropped a new pink eraser. "Just for luck," he said, "not because I expect you to make mistakes."

"Thank you," said the girls.

96

Mrs. Quimby handed each member of the family a lunch and gave Ramona a quick hug. Her father hugged her, too, and said, "Remember, kid, we're counting on you."

When Ramona reached the bus stop, she found Howie Kemp already waiting with his grandmother. The bus, the little yellow school bus Ramona had waited all summer to ride, pulled up at the curb. Ramona and Howie climbed aboard as if they were used to getting on buses by themselves. I did it just like a grown-up, thought Ramona.

"Good morning. I am Mrs. Hanna, your bus aide," said a woman sitting behind the driver. "Take the first empty seats toward the back." Ramona and Howie took window seats on opposite sides of the bus, which had a reassuring new smell.

"By-byee," called Mrs. Kemp, waving as if Ramona and Howie were going on a long, long journey. "By-byee." Howie pretended not to know her.

As soon as the bus pulled away from the curb, Ramona felt someone kick the back of her seat. She turned and faced a sturdy boy wearing a baseball cap with the visor turned up and a white T-shirt with a long word printed across the front. She studied the word to see if she could find short words in it, as she had learned to do in second grade. *Earth. Quakes. Earthquakes.* Some kind of team. Yes, he looked like the sort of boy whose father would take him to ball games.

*Thump, thump, thump* against the back of Ramona's seat. The bus stopped for other children, some excited and some anxious. Still the kicking continued. Ramona ignored it as the bus passed her former school. Good old Glenwood, thought Ramona, as if she had gone there a long, long time ago.

"All right, Danny," said the bus aide to the kicking boy. "As long as I'm riding shotgun on this bus, we won't have anyone kicking the seats. Understand?"

Ramona smiled to herself as she heard Danny mutter an answer. How funny—the bus aide saying she was riding shotgun as if she were guarding a shipment of gold on a stagecoach instead of making children behave on a little yellow school bus.

Ramona pretended she was riding a stagecoach pursued by robbers until she discovered her eraser, her beautiful pink eraser, was missing. "Did you see my eraser?" she asked a second-grade girl, who had taken the seat beside her. The two searched the seat and the floor. No eraser.

Ramona felt a tap on her shoulder and turned. "Was it a pink eraser?" asked the boy in the baseball cap.

"Yes." Ramona was ready to forgive him for kicking her seat. "Have you seen it?"

"Nope." The boy grinned as he jerked down the visor of his baseball cap.

That grin was too much for Ramona. "Liar!" she said with her most ferocious glare, and faced front once more, angry at the loss of her new eraser, angry with herself for dropping it so the boy could find it. Purple cootie, she thought, and hoped the cafeteria would serve him fish portions and those canned green beans with the strings left on. And apple wedges, the soft mushy kind with tough skins, for dessert.

The bus stopped at Cedarhurst, Ramona's new school. As the children hopped out of the bus, Ramona felt a little thrill of triumph. She had not been carsick. She now discovered she felt as if she had grown even more than her feet. Third-graders were the biggest people—except teachers, of course—at this school. All the little first- and second-graders running around the playground, looking so young, made Ramona feel tall, grown-up, and sort of . . . well, wise in the ways of the world.

Danny shoved ahead of her. "Catch!" he yelled to another boy. Something small and pink flew through the air and into the second boy's cupped hands. The boy wound up as if he were pitching a baseball, and the eraser flew back to Danny.

"You gimme back my eraser!" Encumbered by her lunch box, Ramona chased Danny, who ran, ducking and dodging, among the first- and second-graders. When she was about to catch him, he tossed her eraser to the other boy. If her lunch box had not banged against her knees, Ramona might have been able to grab him. Unfortunately, the bell rang first.

"Yard apes!" yelled Ramona, her name for the sort of boys who always got the best balls, who were always first on the playground, and who chased their soccer balls through other people's hopscotch games. She saw her pink eraser fly back into Danny's hands. "Yard apes!" she yelled again, tears of anger in her eyes. "Yucky yard apes!" The boys, of course, paid no attention.

Still fuming, Ramona entered her new school and climbed the stairs to find her assigned classroom. The room was filled with excitement and confusion. She saw some people she had known at her old school. Others were strangers. Everyone was talking at once, shouting greetings to old friends or looking over those who would soon become new friends, rivals, or enemies. Ramona missed Howie,

who had been assigned to another room, but wouldn't you know? That yard ape, Danny, was sitting at a desk, still wearing his baseball cap and tossing Ramona's new eraser from one hand to another. Ramona was too frustrated to speak. She wanted to hit him. How dare he spoil her day?

"All right, you guys, quiet down," said the teacher.

Ramona was startled to hear her class called "you guys." Most teachers she had known would say something like, "I feel I am talking very loud. Is it because the room is noisy?" She chose a chair at a table at the front of the room and studied her new teacher, a strong-looking woman with short hair and a deep tan. Like my swimming teacher, thought Ramona.

"My name is Mrs. Whaley," said the teacher, as she printed her name on the blackboard. "*W-h-a-l-e-y*. I'm a whale with a *y* for a tail." She laughed and so did her class. Then the whale with a *y* for a tail handed Ramona some slips of paper. "Please pass these out," she directed. "We need some name tags until I get to know you."

Ramona did as she was told, and as she walked among the desks she discovered her new sandals squeaked. *Squeak, creak, squeak.*

Ramona giggled, and so did the rest of the class. *Squeak, creak, squeak.* Ramona went up one aisle and down the other. The last person she gave a slip to was the boy from the bus, who was still wearing his baseball cap. "You give me back my eraser, you yard ape!" she whispered.

"Try and get it, Bigfoot," he whispered back with a grin.

Bigfoot indeed! Ramona's feet had grown, but they were not huge. She was not going to let him get away with this insult. "Super-foot to you, Yard Ape," she said right out loud, realizing too late that she had given herself a new nickname.

To her astonishment, Yard Ape pulled her eraser out of his pocket and handed it to her with a grin. Well! With her nose in the air, Ramona squeaked back to her seat. She felt so triumphant that she returned the longest way around and bent her feet as much as she could to make the loudest possible squeaks. She had done the right thing! She had not let Yard Ape upset her by calling her Bigfoot, and now she had her eraser in her hand. He would probably call her Superfoot forever, but she did not care. Superfoot was a name she had given herself. That made all the difference. She had won.

Ramona became aware that she was squeaking in the midst of an unusual silence. She stopped midsqueak when she saw her new teacher watching her with a little smile. The class was watching the teacher.

"We all know you have musical shoes," said Mrs. Whaley. Of course the class laughed.

By walking with stiff legs and not bending her feet, Ramona reached her seat without squeaking at all. She did not know what to think. At first she thought Mrs. Whaley's remark was a reprimand, but then maybe her teacher was just trying to be funny. She couldn't tell about grown-ups sometimes. Ramona finally decided that any teacher who would let Yard Ape wear his baseball cap in the classroom wasn't really fussy about squeaking shoes.

Ramona bent over her paper and wrote slowly and carefully in cursive, Ramona Quimby, age 8. She admired the look of what she had written, and she was happy. She liked feeling tall in her new school. She liked—or was pretty sure she liked—her nonfussy teacher. Yard Ape—Well, he was a problem, but so far she had not let him get the best of her for keeps. Besides, although she might never admit it to anyone, now that she had her eraser back she liked him—sort of. Maybe she enjoyed a challenge.

# Grandparents' Day

GRANDMOTHER TAKES OVER

JEAN VAN LEEUWEN

"Have a nice day," said Mother. "I will be home in time for supper."

Oliver and Amanda waved until they couldn't see Mother anymore. "What is Mother going to do?" asked Oliver.

"She is having a holiday," said Grandmother.

"What is a holiday?" asked Oliver.

"It is a day when you do just what you want to do," said Grandmother.

"I would like to have a holiday," said Oliver.

"Someday you will," said Grandmother. "Now let's have breakfast." Grandmother put Oliver's egg on his plate.

"Something is wrong with my egg," said Oliver. "It's all juicy."

"It is a perfect sunny-side-up egg," said Grandmother.

106

"I don't want a sunny-side-up egg," said Oliver.

"Mother always makes scrambled eggs. With cheese."

Grandmother cooked scrambled eggs with cheese for Oliver and Amanda. She ate the sunny-side-up egg herself.

"What would you like to do today?" asked Grandmother.

"I want to build a road in the dirt for my cars," said Oliver.

"Shall I help you?" asked Grandmother.

"No," said Oliver. "Mother always stays inside. You stay here and clean the house."

For lunch Grandmother made peanut butter sandwiches. "Too much peanut butter," said Oliver. "Mother doesn't put in so much peanut butter."

"The more peanut butter, the better, I always say," said Grandmother. Oliver took a bite. "I'm all full," he said.

After lunch Oliver got out his cars and built a racetrack. Then he got out his blocks and built a city. Then he and Amanda knocked everything down.

"Let's paint pictures," said Oliver.

"First you must clean up this big mess," said Grandmother.

"You help me," said Oliver.

"I can't," said Grandmother. "My knees are too old."

"Mother always helps me," said Oliver. "I want Mother."

"Mama!" Amanda began to cry.

Grandmother held Amanda on her lap in the rocking chair. She sang her a soft song.

"More," said Amanda.

Grandmother sang a song about a sailing ship. And a song about a pig's wig. And a song about the smile on a crocodile.

"Mother never does this," said Oliver, "I like it."

"After you clean up," said Grandmother, "we will sing some more."

When Mother came home, they were still singing. "Did you have a nice day?" asked Mother.

"Yes," said Oliver. "Grandmother made me a perfect sunny-side-up egg and a sandwich with a lot of peanut butter. I cleaned up a big mess myself and we sang songs."

"That sounds very nice," said Mother.

"Grandmother," said Oliver, "will you make me another sunny-side-up egg tomorrow?"

"Not tomorrow," said Grandmother. "Tomorrow I am having a holiday."

### SOME THINGS ABOUT GRANDPAS

Grandfathers *watch* you
They always have time
To see you play baseball
Or jump rope or climb.
Grandpas make whistles
And kites that go high
And boats for your bathtub
And planes that can fly.

Grandfathers *know* things
Like what is a star
And why does it thunder
And how far is far
And grandpas tell stories
With you on their knee
(And there's no other place
That it's nicer to be).

ALICE LOW

# Rosh ha-Shanah

ROSH HA-SHANAH EVE

Stale moon, climb down.
Clear the sky.
Get out of town.
Good-bye.

Fresh moon, arise.
Throw a glow.
Shine a surprise.
Hello

New Year, amen.
Now we begin:
Teach me to be a new me.

HARRY PHILIP

# Columbus Day

CHRISTOPHER COLUMBUS

There are lots of queer things that discoverers do
But his was the queerest, I swear.
He discovered our country in One Four Nine Two
By thinking it couldn't be there.

It wasn't his folly, it wasn't his fault,
For the very best maps of the day
Showed nothing but water, extensive and salt,
On the West, between Spain and Bombay.

There were monsters, of course, every watery mile,
Great krakens with blubbery lips
And sea-serpents smiling a crocodile-smile
As they waited for poor little ships.

There were whirlpools and maelstroms, without any doubt
And tornadoes of lava and ink.
(Which, as nobody yet had been there to find out,
Seems a little bit odd, don't you think?)

But Columbus was bold and Columbus set sail
(Thanks to Queen Isabella, her pelf),
For he said "Though there may be both monster and gale,
I'd like to find out for myself."

And he sailed and he sailed and he *sailed* and he SAILED,
Though his crew would have gladly turned round
And, morning and evening, distressfully wailed
"This is running things into the ground!"

But he paid no attention to protest or squall,
This obstinate son of the mast,
And so, in the end, he discovered us all,
Remarking, "Here's India, at last!"

He didn't intend it, he meant to heave to
At Calcutta, Rangoon or Shanghai,
There are many queer things that discoverers do
But his was the queerest. Oh my!

ROSEMARY CARR AND STEPHEN VINCENT BENÉT

# Halloween

## TEENY-TINY

ENGLISH FOLK TALE

Once upon a time there was a teeny-tiny woman who lived in a teeny-tiny house in a teeny-tiny village. Now, one day this teeny-tiny woman put on her teeny-tiny bonnet and went out of her teeny-tiny house to take a teeny-tiny walk. And when this teeny-tiny woman had gone a teeny-tiny way she came to a teeny-tiny gate, so the teeny-tiny woman opened the teeny-tiny gate, and went into a teeny-tiny churchyard. And when this teeny-tiny woman had got into the teeny-tiny churchyard, she saw a teeny-tiny bone on a teeny-tiny grave, and the teeny-tiny woman said to her teeny-tiny self, "This teeny-tiny bone will make me some teeny-tiny soup for my teeny-tiny supper." So the teeny-tiny woman put the teeny-tiny bone into her teeny-tiny pocket and went home to her teeny-tiny house.

Now when the teeny-tiny woman got home to her teeny-tiny house she was a teeny-tiny bit tired, so she went up her teeny-tiny stairs to her teeny-tiny bed and put the teeny-tiny bone into a teeny-tiny cupboard. And when this teeny-tiny woman had been to sleep a teeny-tiny time, she was awakened by a teeny-tiny voice from the teeny-tiny cupboard, which said:

114

And this teeny-tiny woman was a teeny-tiny frightened, so she hid her teeny-tiny head under the teeny-tiny blankets and went to sleep again. And when she had been to sleep again a teeny-tiny time, the teeny-tiny voice again cried out from the teeny-tiny cupboard a teeny-tiny louder,

## "Give me my bone!"

This made the teeny-tiny woman a teeny-tiny more frightened, so she hid her teeny-tiny head a teeny-tiny further under the teeny-tiny blankets. And when the teeny-tiny woman had been to sleep again a teeny-tiny time, the teeny-tiny voice from the teeny-tiny cupboard said again a teeny-tiny louder,

## "Give me my bone!"

And this teeny-tiny woman was a teeny-tiny bit more frightened, but she put her teeny-tiny head out of the teeny-tiny blankets and said in her loudest teeny-tiny voice,

## . . . THINGS THAT GO BUMP

From Ghoulies and Ghosties,
And long-leggity Beasties,
And all Things that go bump in the Night,
Good Lord deliver us.

FROM A CORNISH LITANY

## THE WITCH! THE WITCH!

The Witch! the Witch! don't let her get you!
Or your Aunt wouldn't know you the next time she met you!

ELEANOR FARJEON

## THREE GHOSTESSES

Three little ghostesses,
Sitting on postesses,
Eating buttered toastesses,
Greasing their fistesses,
Up to their wristesses,
Oh, what beastesses
To make such feastesses!

ANONYMOUS

WITCH GOES SHOPPING

Witch rides off
Upon her broom,
Finds a space
To park it.
Takes a shiny shopping cart
Into the supermarket.
Smacks her lips and reads
The list of things she needs:
 "Six bats' wings,
   Worms in brine,
   Ears of toads,
   Eight or nine.
   Slugs and bugs,
   Snake skins dried,
   Buzzard innards,
   Pickled, fried."
Witch takes herself
From shelf to shelf,
Cackling all the while,
Up and down and up and down and
In and out each aisle.
Out come cans and cartons
Tumbling to the floor.
"This," says Witch, now all a-twitch,
"Is a crazy store.
I CAN'T FIND A SINGLE THING
I AM LOOKING FOR!"

LILIAN MOORE

# ☆☆☆☆ Veterans' Day ☆☆☆☆

THE BIRDS' PEACE

JEAN CRAIGHEAD GEORGE

On the day Kristy's father went off to war, she burst out the back door and ran down the path to the woods. Her eyes hurt. Her chest burned. She crossed the bridge over the purling stream and dashed into the lean-to she and her father had built near the edge of the flower-filled woodland meadow.

She dropped to her knees, then to her belly. Covering her face with both hands, she sobbed from the deepest well of her being.

Tears did not help. The pain went on and on.

A bird sang.

Kristy lifted her head. She recognized Fluter, the busy little song sparrow who lived in the bushes at the edge of the meadow. He seemed to be in trouble. His melodious song was loud and belligerent.

"I'm in trouble, too," she said. "My father had to go into the army. He's going to war. And I am scared." Fluter ignored her and sang on. From across the meadow, a strange song sparrow sang clearly and loudly. Kristy barely heard him.

"Daddy doesn't even know how to shoot a gun."

Fluter flew to a sumac bush, thrust out his spotted tan breast, and sang again.

"Suppose bombs fall on him." Kristy began to cry again. "Or an enemy tank shoots at him."

Fluter went on singing. After a few moments he flew across the meadow and boldly sang from a raspberry patch.

Dulce, his mate, flew off their nest in the thicket, where she had been incubating their eggs. She ate a bristlegrass seed and serenely preened her feathers. She was quite at ease.

Fluter was not. He turned this way and that. He flicked his tail and raised his crest, then flew to the bracken fern and sang. He flitted briskly to the sugar maple limb and sang from a conspicuous twig. He winged to the dogwood tree and sang from a high limb. As he flew and sang, Kristy became aware of what he was doing. He was making a circle, an invisible fence of song around his meadow and his nest in the thicket.

Suddenly Fluter clicked out what Kristy's father had told her were notes of warning. Dulce became alarmed. She flattened her feathers to her body and flew silently back to their nest.

Kristy checked to see what was the matter. The strange song sparrow was in Fluter's raspberry bush. He was pointing his bill at Fluter, who crouched as if he were going to fly at the stranger. But he did not. Instead, he sang.

The stranger heard Fluter's "stay-off-my-property" song and swiftly departed. He flew over Fluter's invisible fence of song and alighted on his own sapling. There he sang at Fluter.

Fluter flew to the sugar maple limb on the border of his territory and sang right back at him. The stranger answered with a flood of melody from his trees and bushes. When each understood where the other's territory lay, they rested and preened their feathers.

Kristy was fascinated. She sat up and crossed her legs.

"Even Daddy doesn't know about this," she said.

Putting her chin in her hands, she watched the birds until the day's long shadows told her she must go home. And all that time, Fluter did not fly or sing beyond the raspberry bush, nor did the stranger come back to Fluter's territory. But sing they did, brightly and melodically, while their mates sat serenely on their brown-splotched eggs.

*Dear Daddy,* Kristy wrote that night.
*I know how the birds keep the peace.*

# Book Week

### THE REASON I LIKE CHOCOLATE

The reason I like chocolate
is I can lick my fingers
and nobody tells me I'm not polite

I especially like scary movies
'cause I can snuggle with Mommy
or my big sister and they don't laugh

I like to cry sometimes 'cause
everybody says "what's the matter
don't cry"

and I like books
for all those reasons
but mostly 'cause they just make me
happy

and I really like
to be happy

NIKKI GIOVANNI

### KEEP A POEM IN YOUR POCKET

Keep a poem in your pocket
and a picture in your head
and you'll never feel lonely
at night when you're in bed.

The little poem will sing to you
the little picture bring to you
a dozen dreams to dance to you
at night when you're in bed.

So—
Keep a picture in your pocket
and a poem in your head
and you'll never feel lonely
at night when you're in bed.

BEATRICE SCHENK DE REGNIERS

### HELLO BOOK!

Hello book!
What are you up to?
Keeping yourself to yourself,
shut in between your covers,
a prisoner high on a shelf.
Come on book!
What is your story?
Haven't you ever been read?
Did you think
    I would just pass by you,
And pick me a comic instead?
No way book!
I'm your reader.
I open you up. Set you free.
    Listen, I know a secret!
    Will you share
        your secrets with me?

N. M. BODECKER

# Thanksgiving

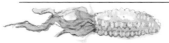 

### THANKSGIVING

Thank You
  for all my hands can hold—
    apples red,
      and melons gold,
        yellow corn
          both ripe and sweet,
            peas and beans
              so good to eat!

Thank You
  for all my eyes can see—
    lovely sunlight,
      field and tree,
        white cloud-boats
          in sea-deep sky,
            soaring bird
              and butterfly.

Thank You
  for all my ears can hear—
    birds' song echoing
      far and near,
        songs of little
          stream, big sea,
            cricket, bullfrog,
              duck and bee!

IVY O. EASTWICK

## THE FIRST THANKSGIVING

When the Pilgrims
first gathered together to share
with their Indian friends
in the mild autumn air,
they lifted their voices
in jubilant praise
for the bread on the table,
the berries and maize,
for field and for forest,
for turkey and deer,
for the bountiful crops
they were blessed with that year.
They were thankful for these
as they feasted away,
and as they were thankful,
we're thankful today.

JACK PRELUTSKY

## THANKSGIVING

I'm glad that I was good today,
    As good as I was able.
I'm glad to be inside this house
    And sitting at this table.

I'm glad that it's Thanksgiving Day
    And all the world is merry,
And I'm glad I have a fork
    And that the pie is cherry.

MARCHETTE CHUTE

125

### THANKSGIVING DAY

Over the river and through the wood,
  To grandfather's house we go;
     The horse knows the way
     To carry the sleigh
  Through the white and drifted snow.

Over the river and through the wood—
  Oh, how the wind does blow!
     It stings the toes
     And bites the nose,
  As over the ground we go.

Over the river and through the wood,
  To have a first-rate play.
     Hear the bells ring,
     "Ting-a-ling-ding!"
  Hurrah for Thanksgiving Day!

Over the river and through the wood,
  Trot fast, my dapple-gray!
     Spring over the ground,
     Like a hunting-hound!
  For this is Thanksgiving Day.

Over the river and through the wood,
  And straight through the barn-yard gate.
     We seem to go
     Extremely slow—
  It is so hard to wait!

Over the river and through the wood—
  Now grandmother's cap I spy!
     Hurrah for the fun!
     Is the pudding done?
  Hurrah for the pumpkin-pie!

L. MARIA CHILD

#  Hanukkah

## POTATO PANCAKES ALL AROUND

MARILYN HIRSH

On a cold winter afternoon, Samuel the peddler walked down the road to a village. He passed children sliding and sledding and skating.

"The children are out of school early," he said to himself, "because tonight is the first night of Hanukkah."

When Samuel reached the village, it was almost dark. He knocked on the door of a house. Mama opened the door and smiled at the peddler.

"A guest is always welcome," she said. "Come in. We are just lighting the first candle."

So they all sang the blessings together. The two grandmothers went to the stove.

128

"Aha," thought Samuel, "now they'll start making potato pancakes."

"We'll use my recipe," Grandma Yetta said firmly.

"No, mine is better!" answered Grandma Sophie.

"Who needs recipes?" said Samuel the peddler. "I'll show you how to make potato pancakes from a crust of bread!"

"Some say for potato pancakes a pickle, a fish, or a cabbage is good," Samuel continued, "but I say a crust of bread is best."

"Ridiculous," said Grandma Yetta.

"That's crazy," said Grandma Sophie.

"We're hungry!" cried the twins.

"So let's try the peddler's idea," said Mama.

Samuel took a bowl from his sack. "Who wants to hold it?" he asked.

"We do!" yelled the twins.

Samuel carefully grated a crust of bread into the bowl. "It looks delicious," he announced. "But it needs a little water."

The grandmothers wouldn't even look.

The peddler tasted the batter. "Some would say it needs salt . . . a little pepper, perhaps?"

"Even I know it needs salt and pepper," said Papa.

"Well, if you insist, I wouldn't say no," replied the peddler. And he added salt and pepper.

Samuel noticed a chicken looking in the window. "I think this chicken is trying to tell me something. But what could a chicken say?"

"I know!" cried Rachel. "The chicken is telling you to add eggs."

"I have heard of that," agreed the peddler. And he added six eggs.

"He takes advice from chickens," said Grandma Yetta.

"Do *you* have any suggestions?" he asked her politely.

"May you grow like an onion with your head in the ground!" she shouted.

"Ah, onions! A good idea," said Samuel.

So David hurried to chop some onions.

Samuel smiled. "Any minute now, we'll have potato pancakes."

"But what about the potatoes?" asked Sarah. "I grated all these potatoes, all by myself."

"It's not in my recipe," said Samuel, "but it's a sin to waste food. So what can it hurt? I'll add your potatoes." And he did.

"What will you fry the potato pancakes in?" asked Grandma Yetta and Grandma Sophie at the same time.

"In a frying pan," answered Samuel. And he took one from his sack.

"Chicken fat is best," insisted Grandma Yetta.

"You may be right," said Samuel.

"Goose fat is better," declared Grandma Sophie.

"I wouldn't say no," Samuel replied.

So Samuel took a big spoonful of chicken fat and a big spoonful of goose fat and began to fry the potato pancakes. Delicious smells filled the house. Samuel kept on frying. More and more potato pancakes piled up. Finally, it was time to eat. So they ate and ate and ate potato pancakes all around. Even Grandma Yetta and Grandma Sophie agreed that the potato pancakes were the best ever.

And they danced. And they sang. And they played games until very late. Grandma Yetta and Grandma Sophie gave the children pennies. Then everyone went to sleep.

The next morning, the family begged Samuel to stay for the whole eight days of Hanukkah.

"Thank you," said Samuel, "but a peddler must move along. I know you'll have a happy Hanukkah, now that you can make potato pancakes from a crust of bread."

# Christmas

DEAR SANTA CLAUS

Dear Santa Claus,

It's me again
reminding you I'm here,
I'm making my list easier
and shorter than last year.

I'd like a stack of comic books,
a dozen apple pies,
a box of chocolate brownies,
and an elephant that flies,

a porpoise for the bathtub
and a dragon for my room,
a robot that does homework
and can also use a broom.

And I'd like a hippopotamus,
a trumpet, and a drum,
I could use a half a dollar
and a million sticks of gum.

Just leave them underneath our tree
or near our fireplace,
Oh! you probably won't bring them,
but I'm writing . . . just in case.

JACK PRELUTSKY

134

## CHRISTMAS

My goodness, my goodness,
It's Christmas again.
The bells are all ringing.
I do not know when
I've been so excited.
The tree is all fixed,
The candles are lighted,
The pudding is mixed.

The wreath's on the door
And the carols are sung,
The presents are wrapped
And the holly is hung.
The turkey is sitting
All safe in its pan,
And I am behaving
As calm as I can.

MARCHETTE CHUTE

135

## Mr. Edwards Meets Santa Claus

LAURA INGALLS WILDER

The days were short and cold, the wind whistled sharply, but there was no snow. Cold rains were falling. Day after day the rain fell, pattering on the roof and pouring from the eaves.

Mary and Laura stayed close by the fire, sewing their nine-patch quilt blocks, or cutting paper dolls from scraps of wrapping-paper, and hearing the wet sound of the rain. Every night was so cold that they expected to see snow next morning, but in the morning they saw only sad, wet grass.

They pressed their noses against the squares of glass in the windows that Pa had made, and they were glad they could see out. But they wished they could see snow.

Laura was anxious because Christmas was near, and Santa Claus and his reindeer could not travel without snow. Mary was afraid that, even if it snowed, Santa Claus could not find them, so far away in Indian Territory. When they asked Ma about this, she said she didn't know.

136

"What day is it?" they asked her, anxiously. "How many more days till Christmas?" And they counted off the days on their fingers, till there was only one more day left.

Rain was still falling that morning. There was not one crack in the gray sky. They felt almost sure there would be no Christmas. Still, they kept hoping.

Just before noon the light changed. The clouds broke and drifted apart, shining white in a clear blue sky. The sun shone, birds sang, and thousands of drops of water sparkled on the grasses. But when Ma opened the door to let in the fresh, cold air, they heard the creek roaring.

They had not thought about the creek. Now they knew they would have no Christmas, because Santa Claus could not cross that roaring creek.

Pa came in, bringing a big fat turkey. If it weighed less than twenty pounds, he said, he'd eat it, feathers and all. He asked Laura, "How's that for a Christmas dinner? Think you can manage one of those drumsticks?"

She said, yes, she could. But she was sober. Then Mary asked him if the creek was going down, and he said it was still rising.

Ma said it was too bad. She hated to think of Mr. Edwards eating his bachelor cooking all alone on Christmas day. Mr. Edwards had been asked to eat Christmas dinner with them, but Pa shook his head and said a man would risk his neck, trying to cross that creek now.

"No," he said, "That current's too strong. We'll just have to make up our minds that Edwards won't be here tomorrow."

Of course that meant that Santa Claus could not come, either.

Laura and Mary tried not to mind too much. They watched Ma dress the wild turkey, and it was a very fat turkey. They were lucky little girls, to have a good house to live in, and a warm fire to sit by, and such a turkey for their Christmas dinner. Ma said so, and it was true. Ma said it was too bad that Santa Claus couldn't come this year, but they were such good girls that he hadn't forgotten them; he would surely come next year.

Still, they were not happy.

After supper that night they washed their hands and faces, buttoned their red-flannel nightgowns, tied their night-cap strings, and soberly said their prayers. They lay down in bed and pulled the covers up. It did not seem at all like Christmas time.

Pa and Ma sat silent by the fire. After a while Ma asked why Pa didn't play the fiddle, and he said, "I don't seem to have the heart to, Caroline."

After a longer while, Ma suddenly stood up.

"I'm going to hang up your stockings, girls," she said. "Maybe something will happen."

Laura's heart jumped. But then she thought again of the creek and she knew nothing could happen.

Ma took one of Mary's clean stockings and one of Laura's, and she hung them from the mantel-shelf, on either side of the fireplace. Laura and Mary watched her over the edge of their bedcovers.

"Now go to sleep," Ma said, kissing them goodnight. "Morning will come quicker if you're asleep."

She sat down again by the fire and Laura almost went to sleep. She woke up a little when she heard Pa say, "You've only made it worse, Caroline." And she thought she heard Ma say: "No, Charles. There's the white sugar." But perhaps she was dreaming.

Then she heard Jack growl savagely. The door-latch rattled and someone said, "Ingalls! Ingalls!" Pa was stirring up the fire, and when he opened the door Laura saw that it was morning. The outdoors was gray.

"Great fishhooks, Edwards! Come in, man! What's happened?" Pa exclaimed.

Laura saw the stockings limply dangling, and she scrooged her shut eyes into the pillow. She heard Pa piling wood on the fire, and she heard Mr. Edwards say he had carried his clothes on his head when he swam the creek. His teeth rattled and his voice shivered. He would be all right, he said, as soon as he got warm.

"It was too big a risk, Edwards," Pa said. "We're glad you're here, but that was too big a risk for a Christmas dinner."

"Your little ones had to have a Christmas," Mr. Edwards replied. "No creek could stop me, after I fetched them their gifts from Independence."

Laura sat straight up in bed. "Did you see Santa Claus?" she shouted.

"I sure did," Mr. Edwards said.

"Where? When? What did he look like? What did he say? Did he really give you something for us?" Mary and Laura cried.

"Wait, wait a minute!" Mr. Edwards laughed. And Ma said she would put the presents in the stockings, as Santa Claus intended. She said they mustn't look.

Mr. Edwards came and sat on the floor by their bed, and he answered every question they asked him. They honestly tried not to look at Ma, and they didn't quite see what she was doing.

When he saw the creek rising, Mr. Edwards said, he had known that Santa Claus could not get across it. ("But you crossed it," Laura said. "Yes," Mr. Edwards replied, "but Santa Claus is too old and fat. He couldn't make it, where a long, lean razor-back like me could do so.") And Mr. Edwards reasoned that if Santa Claus couldn't cross the creek, likely he would come no farther south than Independence. Why should he come forty miles across the prairie, only to be turned back? Of course he wouldn't do that!

So Mr. Edwards had walked to Independence. ("In the rain?" Mary asked. Mr. Edwards said he wore his rubber coat.) And there, coming down the street in Independence, he had met Santa Claus. ("In the daytime?" Laura asked. She hadn't thought that anyone could see Santa Claus in the daytime. No, Mr. Edwards said; it was night, but light shone out across the street from the saloons.)

Well, the first thing Santa Claus said was, "Hello, Edwards!" ("Did he know you?" Mary asked, and Laura asked, "How did you know he was really Santa Claus?" Mr. Edwards said that Santa Claus knew everybody. And he had recognized Santa at once by his whiskers. Santa Claus had the longest, thickest, whitest set of whiskers west of the Mississippi.)

So Santa Claus said, "Hello, Edwards! Last time I saw you you were sleeping on a corn-shuck bed in Tennessee." And Mr. Edwards well remembered the little pair of red-yarn mittens that Santa Claus had left for him that time.

Then Santa Claus said: "I understand you're living now down along the Verdigris River. Have you ever met up, down yonder, with two little young girls named Mary and Laura?"

"I surely am acquainted with them," Mr. Edwards replied.

"It rests heavy on my mind," said Santa Claus. "They are both of them sweet, pretty, good little young things, and I know they are expecting me. I surely do hate to disappoint two good little girls like them. Yet with the water up the way it is, I can't ever make it across that creek. I can figure no way whatsoever to get to their cabin this year. Edwards," Santa Claus said. "Would you do me the favor to fetch them their gifts this one time?"

"I'll do that, and with pleasure," Mr. Edwards told him.

Then Santa Claus and Mr. Edwards stepped across the street to the hitching-posts where the pack-mule was tied. ("Didn't he have his reindeer?" Laura asked. "You know he couldn't," Mary said. "There isn't any snow." Exactly, said Mr. Edwards. Santa Claus traveled with a pack-mule in the southwest.)

And Santa Claus uncinched the pack and looked through it, and he took out the presents for Mary and Laura.

"Oh, what are they?" Laura cried; but Mary asked, "Then what did he do?"

Then he shook hands with Mr. Edwards, and he swung up on his fine bay horse. Santa Claus rode well, for a man of his weight and build. And he tucked his long, white whiskers under his bandana. "So long, Edwards," he said, and he rode away on the Fort Dodge trail, leading his pack-mule and whistling.

Laura and Mary were silent an instant, thinking of that.

Then Ma said, "You may look now, girls."

Something was shining bright in the top of Laura's stocking. She squealed and jumped out of bed. So did Mary, but Laura beat her to the fireplace. And the shining thing was a glittering new tin cup.

Mary had one exactly like it.

These new tin cups were their very own. Now they each had a cup to drink out of. Laura jumped up and down and shouted and laughed, but Mary stood still and looked with shining eyes at her own tin cup.

Then they plunged their hands into the stockings again. And they pulled out two long, long sticks of candy. It was peppermint candy, striped red and white. They looked and looked at that beautiful candy, and Laura licked her stick, just one lick. But Mary was not so greedy. She didn't take even one lick of her stick.

Those stockings weren't empty yet. Mary and Laura pulled out two small packages. They unwrapped them, and each found a little heart-shaped cake. Over their delicate brown tops was sprinkled white sugar. The sparkling grains lay like tiny drifts of snow.

The cakes were too pretty to eat. Mary and Laura just looked at them. But at last Laura turned hers over, and she nibbled a tiny nibble from underneath, where it wouldn't show. And the inside of that little cake was white!

It had been made of pure white flour, and sweetened with white sugar.

Laura and Mary never would have looked in their stockings again. The cups and the cakes and the candy were almost too much. They were too happy to speak. But Ma asked if they were sure the stockings were empty.

Then they put their arms down inside them, to make sure.

And in the very toe of each stocking was a shining bright, new penny!

They had never even thought of such a thing as having a penny. Think of having a whole penny for your very own. Think of having a cup and a cake and a stick of candy *and* a penny.

There never had been such a Christmas.

Now of course, right away, Laura and Mary should have thanked Mr. Edwards for bringing those lovely presents all the way from Independence. But they had forgotten all about Mr. Edwards. They had even forgotten Santa Claus. In a minute they would have remembered, but before they did, Ma said, gently, "Aren't you going to thank Mr. Edwards?"

"Oh, thank you, Mr. Edwards! Thank you!" they said, and they meant it with all their hearts. Pa shook Mr. Edwards' hand, too, and shook it again. Pa and Ma and Mr. Edwards acted as if they were almost crying, Laura didn't know why. So she gazed again at her beautiful presents.

She looked up again when Ma gasped. And Mr. Edwards was taking sweet potatoes out of his pockets. He said they had helped to balance the package on his head when he swam across the creek. He thought Pa and Ma might like them, with the Christmas turkey.

There were nine sweet potatoes. Mr. Edwards had brought them all the way from town, too. It was just too much. Pa said so. "It's too much, Edwards," he said. They never could thank him enough.

Mary and Laura were too much excited to eat breakfast. They drank the milk from their shining new cups, but they could not swallow the rabbit stew and the cornmeal mush.

"Don't make them, Charles," Ma said. "It will soon be dinnertime."

For Christmas dinner there was the tender, juicy, roasted turkey. There were the sweet potatoes, baked in the ashes and carefully wiped so that you could eat the good skins, too. There was a loaf of salt-rising bread made from the last of the white flour.

And after all that there were stewed dried blackberries and little cakes. But these little cakes were made with brown sugar and they did not have white sugar sprinkled over their tops.

Then Pa and Ma and Mr. Edwards sat by the fire and talked about Christmas times back in Tennessee and up north in the Big Woods. But Mary and Laura looked at their beautiful cakes and played with their pennies and drank water out of their new cups. And little by little they licked and sucked their sticks of candy, till each stick was sharp-pointed on one end.

That was a happy Christmas.

## GO TELL IT ON THE MOUNTAIN

Go tell it on the mountain,
Over the hills and everywhere;
Go tell it on the mountain,
That Jesus Christ is born.

Down in a lowly manger
The humble Christ was born;
And God sent out salvation
That blessed Christmas morn.

Go tell it on the mountain,
Over the hills and everywhere;
Go tell it on the mountain,
That Jesus Christ is born.

**SPIRITUAL**

## WATCH

The lamb baaed gently.
The tender donkey showed its joy
in lusty bray.
The dog barked playfully
almost talking to the stars.

I could not sleep. I went outdoors
and saw heavenly tracks upon the ground
all flower-decked
like a sky
turned upside down.

A warm and fragrant mist
hovered over the grove;
the moon was sinking low
in a soft golden west
of divine orbit.

My breast beat without pause,
as if my heart had wined . . .

I opened wide the stable door to
see if He were there.
     He was!

JUAN RAMÓN JIMÉNEZ,
TRANSLATED BY ELOISE ROACH

### OH CALENDAR

To see
December press
Its face against the door,
I realize I've grown an inch
Or more

Since we
First hung you up.
You measured time by turns:
Hard winter nights to softball days,
Sunburns,

The chill
At Halloween,
Then! rumors of reindeer
Across the sky. Good-bye, Happy
Old Year!

J. PATRICK LEWIS

# The Holidays

**NEW YEAR'S DAY**—January 1
January 1 was first celebrated as the beginning of the New Year in 153 B.C., when the Romans decided to begin their calendar on that day. It was officially adopted in the sixteenth century in Europe, when Pope Gregory XIII introduced a revised calendar, and is now the start of the secular year throughout the world. The month January is named for the Roman god Janus, who had two faces, one looking back and the other looking ahead.

**CHINESE NEW YEAR**
There is more than one calendar in the world, although the Gregorian calendar, in use in the West since the sixteenth century, is used by almost every country for conducting business and government. Chinese New Year comes on the first day of the first moon, as the Chinese call their months, usually in February. It is a day of visiting, feasting, and parades, led by a great twisting, weaving dragon. There are firecrackers, too. New Year's Day is also the day to celebrate everybody's birthday, according to Chinese tradition.

**MARTIN LUTHER KING DAY**—Third Monday in January
Martin Luther King Day commemorates the birthday of a great American, Martin Luther King, Jr., who was born on January 15, 1929. A black minister from Atlanta, Georgia, he led the struggle for racial equality in the United States. Dr. King believed in nonviolence, and he preached passive resistance. His first major protest was a boycott of the Montgomery, Alabama, buses because blacks had to sit in the back. In 1964 he won the Nobel Peace Prize. People all over the world were shocked and saddened when he was assassinated at the age of thirty-nine.

**VALENTINE'S DAY**—February 14
On St. Valentine's Day people send gifts and cards to their friends. The cards often sport a bright red heart, the symbol of love and affection. Nobody is sure how this holiday began, but there are several stories about it. One is that it is based on an ancient Roman festival, Lupercalia, when young men drew young women's names out of a box to be their partners at a feast in February. Another is based on the mating of birds, said to occur on February 14.

**PRESIDENTS' DAY**—Third Monday in February
Presidents' Day celebrates the birthdays of two of the greatest presidents of the United States— Abraham Lincoln, who was born on February 12, 1809, and George Washington, who was born on February 22, 1732. Some states still celebrate the birthdays separately.

Abraham Lincoln, one of the greatest presidents of the United States, was born in a cabin on a farm in Kentucky. He became a lawyer, then a congressman, and was elected the sixteenth president of the United States in 1860. In 1861 the Civil War between the states of the American North and the American South began. Under Lincoln's leadership the North won the war, and the United States became one country again. The question of whether slavery was legal was a major issue of the war; in 1863 Lincoln freed the slaves in his Emancipation Proclamation. Reelected in 1864, Lincoln was assassinated, on April 14, 1865.

George Washington, the first president of the United States, was born on a plantation in Virginia in 1732 to a wealthy family. When the Revolutionary War against Great Britain began, Washington was named Commander-in-Chief of the American army and led the thirteen colonies to victory and independence. After the war he presided over the Constitutional Convention, which drew up the Constitution of the United States. In 1789 he was unanimously chosen the first president of the new country and served two terms. At his funeral in 1799 a friend declared he was "first in war, first in peace, and first in the hearts of his countrymen."

**ST. PATRICK'S DAY**—March 17
March 17 is said to be the day Patrick, Ireland's patron saint, died. When he was a young man, Patrick was captured and sold as a slave. He later escaped to France, where he rose to the position of bishop. When he returned he brought Christianity with him to Ireland, founding many churches and schools. The Irish and their descendants all over the world celebrate this day by wearing green, sporting a shamrock, and marching in parades.

**APRIL FOOL'S DAY**—April 1

Have you ever wondered how the custom of playing jokes on April 1 began? In Europe, up to the sixteenth century, March 25 was the beginning of the New Year. It was marked by an eight-day celebration ending April 1, when people visited and gave each other presents. When the countries in Europe changed the calendar and made January 1 the start of the New Year, many people continued these April 1 customs. They were called April fools.

**PASSOVER**—Eight days beginning the fifteenth day
of the Hebrew month Nissan, usually in March or April

Passover celebrates the Exodus, or escape, of the Jews from Egypt over three thousand years ago and their freedom from slavery to Pharaoh, the leader of the Egyptians. The Bible tells us that to convince the Egyptians to let the Jewish people go, God visited terrible plagues on the Egyptians. But Pharaoh would not yield. Moses, the leader of the Jews, then told Pharaoh that a final awful plague would descend on Egypt: God would kill the firstborn son of every Egyptian family. To let God know which families to spare, the Jews sacrificed a lamb and sprinkled some of its blood on the doorposts of their houses so the Angel of Death would "pass over" them. Pharaoh was convinced and let the Jews go.

Jews commemorate this escape from bondage with a seder. At this holiday meal they retell the story of the Exodus, sing Passover songs, and eat traditional foods. One of these is matzo—flat, unleavened bread that, like crackers, has not risen. It reminds Jews that their ancestors left Egypt so hastily that they did not have time to let their bread rise.

**EASTER**—First Sunday after the first full moon
after the spring equinox; later in Orthodox churches

Easter, the most joyous and solemn Christian holiday, celebrates the resurrection of Jesus. According to the Gospels, Jesus disappeared from the tomb where he was buried and rose from the dead on the third day after he had been crucified, a miracle that signified the triumph of life over death and held out the hope of rebirth. Easter climaxes almost eight weeks of fasting and holy days, called Lent, which begin with Ash Wednesday. Easter Sunday is celebrated in churches around the world, often with music and flowers, especially lilies.

The word *Easter* may come from the Anglo-Saxon name for the goddess of spring and fertility, Eostra. Long before Christianity, a spring festival welcomed the rebirth of nature, when grass and flowers grow, trees bud and leaf, and birds return. Eostra's symbol was a hare, which may explain the Easter bunny and the basket of eggs. Eggs are a symbol of birth and for a long time were not eaten during Lent; the Easter bunny brings them back. Eggs were colored in Egypt and Persia for the festival of spring, and the custom was probably brought to Europe by traders and travelers.

**EARTH DAY**—April 22

Earth Day was established in 1970 to "give the Earth a chance." There is only one planet Earth, and we must all work to make sure it survives. Earth Day gives us a chance to think about how to protect our air, our oceans and rivers, and every living thing.

**ARBOR DAY**—Varies state by state in the United States
and province by province in Canada, but usually last Friday in April

On April 10, 1872, J. Sterling Morton, a newspaper editor who was interested in conservation, talked the Nebraska agricultural board into setting aside a day to plant trees. Nebraska had almost no trees, and Morton thought they would not only help prevent erosion but be beautiful. In 1885, April 22, Morton's birthday, Arbor Day was made a legal holiday, and soon it was celebrated across the United States and Canada.

**MOTHER'S DAY**—Second Sunday in May

The day that honors mothers was first celebrated in 1908, at the suggestion of Anna Jarvis, whose mother had died the year before. It is observed in many countries around the world.

**MEMORIAL DAY**—Observed on the last Monday in May

Memorial Day began during the Civil War, when women decorated with flowers the graves of soldiers who had died in that long and divisive struggle between the American North and the American South. For that reason it was first called Decoration Day. Today, people in the United States remember and honor the dead of all its wars on this day.

**HAPPY BIRTHDAY**—Every day and one special day

Everybody has a birthday, so we all get to celebrate our own very special day with a party, cake, games, and presents. Many of these customs started long ago in Europe to ward off evil spirits and keep a person safe or lucky for the coming year.

**FATHER'S DAY**—Third Sunday in June
Father's Day was first celebrated in Spokane, Washington, in 1910. Sonora Louise Smart Dodd was inspired to call for a day honoring fathers because of her own father, who brought up his six children after his wife died in childbirth. It is observed in the United States and Canada.

**CANADA DAY**—July 1
On July 1, 1867, the British North America Act united four provinces of Canada into a country and made it a British dominion. The Canadians won a large degree of self-government and representation in the British Parliament. Later other provinces joined the union. Canadians celebrate the birthday of Canada with picnics, parades, and fireworks.

**INDEPENDENCE DAY**—July 4
July 4 celebrates the birthday of the United States. All over the country there are parades, picnics, fireworks, band concerts, and the ringing of bells. On July 4, 1776, the Declaration of Independence, written by Thomas Jefferson, was approved by the Continental Congress in Philadelphia. It stated that the thirteen American colonies were free and independent of England and proclaimed the right of each citizen to life, liberty, and the pursuit of happiness.

**FRIENDSHIP DAY**—August 4
On this day we should all let our friends know how much we care about them. Of course, we should do this every day, but it's good to have a day set aside to remind everyone how important our friends are.

**LABOR DAY**—First Monday in September
Labor Day, celebrated in the United States, Puerto Rico, and Canada, honors workers with a day off and informally marks the end of summer vacation time. Labor Day was first observed as a national holiday in 1894 to call attention to the contribution that laborers and factory workers made to their country.

**GRANDPARENTS' DAY**—First Sunday after Labor Day or September 8
This day was started by Marian McQuade to honor grandparents. If your grandparents live nearby, you can give them a special hug. If they live far away, you can send them a note or call them to tell them that you miss them.

**ROSH HA-SHANAH**—First day of the Hebrew month Tishri, usually in September
Rosh ha-Shanah means the head, or beginning, of the year and marks the start of the Jewish High Holy Days, which end with Yom Kippur. This is a solemn time. On Rosh ha-Shanah a ram's horn, or shofar, is blown to "awaken" Jews to think about how they have behaved in the year that is ending and how they will behave in the new year. Meals often include honey and apples, to bring sweetness to the New Year, and holiday loaves are baked in a spiral shape, which shows that the year comes around to a fresh start.

**COLUMBUS DAY**—October 12; observed on the second Monday in October
On October 12, 1492, Christopher Columbus discovered the New World. This date has been celebrated for centuries by parades in North and South America, as well as in Italy, where Columbus was born, and in Spain, where he started his voyage. Columbus believed that by sailing west he would find a shorter route than the long trip around Africa to the Indies and their rich spices. He convinced King Ferdinand and Queen Isabella of Spain, and they supplied him with three ships, the *Niña*, the *Pinta*, and the *Santa Maria*, to sail across the vast, uncharted Atlantic Ocean. When at last his ships landed on the island of San Salvador in the Bahamas, Columbus thought he had reached the East Indies. For this reason, he called the people who greeted him Indians; today we call them Native Americans.

**HALLOWEEN**—October 31
Long before children celebrated Halloween by dressing up as ghosts and witches, trick or treating, and carving pumpkins, it was the night before All Saints' Day, a Christian holy day in Great Britain and Ireland. *Hallowed* means holy, and *een* is short for evening. And long before *that,* the Celtic people of the British Isles celebrated a harvest festival called Samhain, in honor of the dead. The Celts believed that the spirits of the dead, in the form of ghosts and goblins, gathered that night. Masked, costumed people helped frighten them away, and witches had magic powers on that evening.

**VETERANS DAY**—November 11
On November 11, 1918, an armistice was declared between the Central and Allied powers, ending World War I. This day is now celebrated in England; Canada, where it is called Remembrance Day; and France to honor all those who fell in World War I and World War II. In 1954

the United States changed the name of this day to Veterans Day to commemorate all those men and women who served in the armed forces in all U.S. wars.

**BOOK WEEK**—Third week in November

During National Children's Book Week everyone connected with books—writers, illustrators, librarians, publishers, booksellers, teachers, parents, and children—celebrates the many pleasures of reading. The spark for Book Week was lit in 1912, when E. W. Mumford, a publisher, made a speech that warned against the dangers of children's reading only silly, junky books. The speech attracted the attention of a Boy Scout leader, who in turn won the cooperation of booksellers and librarians in sponsoring Good Book Week in 1916. Today National Children's Book Week is sponsored by the Children's Book Council.

**THANKSGIVING**—Second Monday in October in Canada,

Fourth Thursday in November in the United States

People in many parts of the world have a feast in the fall to give thanks for the harvest. In Canada and the United States it is called Thanksgiving.

Thanksgiving came to Canada with settlers from the United States and has been an official holiday since 1879. Churches are decorated with the fruits of the harvest, and there are bountiful dinners.

Thanksgiving in the United States commemorates that first harvest feast of the Pilgrims in Plymouth, Massachusetts, in 1621. The survivors of the trip from England on the *Mayflower* had settled there and endured a long, hard winter with little to eat. In the spring an Indian named Squanto helped the Pilgrims plant barley and corn. When they harvested their crops, the governor of the little colony declared a day of thanksgiving and invited the Indians who had befriended the colonists to share in the feast. Thanksgiving was celebrated off and on in colonial times. President Washington proclaimed a national Thanksgiving after the American Revolution, and President Lincoln revived the custom during the Civil War. In 1941 Congress fixed Thanksgiving on the fourth Thursday in November.

**HANUKKAH**—Eight days beginning the twenty-fifth day

of the Hebrew month Kislev, usually in December

The word *Hanukkah* means dedication, and the eight days of this Jewish holiday recall the rededication of the Temple in Jerusalem after the Jews triumphed over the Syrian king Antiochus IV. In 165 B.C. Antiochus had conquered Jerusalem and forced the Jews to worship foreign gods. Led by Judah Maccabee, they fought a war so they could worship freely again.

After the Jews cleaned the foreign gods out of the Temple, they wanted to light the new menorah, a candelabrum, to rededicate the Temple, but they had only enough oil to burn for one day. Miraculously the oil lasted for eight days. To recall this miracle, Jews light a Hanukkah menorah—one candle the first night, two the second—until all eight are lit. Families also sing songs, exchange little presents—often coins—and play games, especially one with a top called a dreydel.

**CHRISTMAS**—December 25

Christmas is one of the most important and happy occasions of the Christian year, for it celebrates the birth of Jesus. According to the Gospels of the New Testament, he was born to Mary in a stable in Bethlehem since there was no room for them at the inn. At his birth angels announced the coming of the savior to shepherds who were tending their flocks, and a brilliant star shone in the east. Three wise men followed the star, and it led them to the manger in Bethlehem where the baby Jesus was lying. They brought him gifts and worshiped him.

Christmas is a religious holiday, celebrated in church services throughout the world. It is also a holiday that draws on many winter festivals that were celebrated before Jesus was born. Gifts are a Roman tradition, and evergreen, mistletoe, and holly are also ancient winter decorations. The beautiful music of Christmas can be heard in carols. For children Christmas is the time when Santa Claus comes down the chimney to fill stockings in the United States, when the Three Kings bring gifts to children in Spanish-speaking countries, and Saint Nicholas brings gifts to Dutch and Belgian children. On Boxing Day, December 26, everyone relaxes in Canada, England, and several other countries. This day off has come down from the nineteenth century, when families used to give Christmas boxes to the postman and other service people on the day after Christmas.

# Acknowledgments

Every effort has been made to ascertain the ownership of all copyrighted material and to secure the necessary permissions. In the event of any questions arising as to the use of any material, the editor and the publisher, while expressing regret for any inadvertent error, will be happy to make the necessary correction in future printings.

"My Own Day." From LOOK THROUGH MY WINDOW by Jean Little. Copyright © 1970. Reprinted by permission of HarperCollins Publishers.

"Dream Variations." From SELECTED POEMS OF LANGSTON HUGHES. Copyright © 1926 by Alfred A. Knopf, Inc., renewed © 1954 by Langston Hughes. Reprinted by permission of Alfred A. Knopf, Inc.

"Beginning a New Year Means" by Ruth Whitman. Copyright © 1987 by Ruth Whitman. Reprinted by permission of the author.

"Bouquet of Roses." From LAS NAVIDADES, selected and illustrated by Lulu Delacre. Copyright © 1990. Reprinted by permission of Scholastic, Inc.

"Chinese New Year." From CHINESE MOTHER GOOSE RHYMES. Copyright © 1968 by Robert Wyndham. Reprinted by permission of Philomel Books.

"We Shall Overcome," Verses 1, 2, and 8, by Zilphia Horton, Frank Hamilton, Guy Carawan, and Pete Seeger (TRO). Copyright renewed © 1960, 1963 by Ludlow Music, Inc. Used by permission.

"Dreams." From THE DREAMKEEPER AND OTHER POEMS by Langston Hughes. Copyright © 1932 by Alfred A. Knopf, Inc., renewed © 1960 by Langston Hughes. Reprinted by permission of Alfred A. Knopf, Inc.

"I Made My Dog a Valentine." From IT'S VALENTINE'S DAY by Jack Prelutsky. Copyright © 1983 by Jack Prelutsky. Reprinted by permission of Greenwillow Books, William Morrow & Co., Inc.

"The Porcupine" by Karla Kuskin. From Cricket, the Magazine for Children. Copyright © 1974 by Karla Kuskin. Reprinted by permission of the author.

"Abraham Lincoln" and "Christopher Columbus." From A BOOK OF AMERICANS by Rosemary Carr and Stephen Vincent Benét, Holt, Rinehart & Winston, Inc. Copyright © 1933 by Rosemary and Stephen Vincent Benét; renewed © 1961 by Rosemary Carr Benét. Reprinted by permission of Brandt & Brandt Literary Agents, Inc.

"George Washington's Breakfast" by Jean Fritz. Copyright © 1969 by Jean Fritz. Abridged; reprinted by permission of Coward, McCann & Geoghegan.

"The Hungry Leprechaun" by Mary Calhoun. Copyright 1961, 1962 by Mary Calhoun, © renewed 1989, 1990. Reprinted by permission of William Morrow & Company.

"Arthur's April Fool" by Marc Brown. Copyright © 1983 by Marc Brown. Reprinted by permission of Little, Brown and Co.

"The Magician." From IN THIS WORLD AND THE NEXT by Isaac L. Peretz, translated by Moshe Spiegel. Reprinted by permission of Associated University Press.

"Patience" by Bobbi Katz. Copyright © 1979 by Bobbi Katz. Reprinted by permission of the author.

"The Easter Parade." From LAUGHING TIME by William Jay Smith. Copyright © 1955, 1957, 1980, 1990 by William Jay Smith. Reprinted by permission of Farrar, Straus and Giroux, Inc.

"The Sun on Easter Day" by Norma Farber. From EASTER POEMS by Myra Cohn Livingston. Copyright © 1985 by Norma Farber. Reprinted by permission of Tom Farber.

"A Lamb on the Table" by Concetta C. Doucette. From Cricket, the Magazine for Children. Copyright © 1985. Reprinted by permission of the author.

"Thinking Green." From 50 SIMPLE THINGS KIDS CAN DO TO SAVE THE EARTH. Copyright © 1989, John Javna, The Earthworks Group. Reprinted by permission of Andrews and McMeel Publishers.

"Blow-up." From THE FORGETFUL WISHING WELL by X. J. Kennedy. Copyright © 1985 by X. J. Kennedy. Reprinted by permission of Margaret K. McElderry Books, an imprint of Macmillan Publishing Company.

"Trees" by Nelda Dishman from MIRACLES: POEMS BY CHILDREN OF THE ENGLISH-SPEAKING WORLD. Originally published by Simon & Schuster, © 1966. Published in 1991 by The Touchstone Center, © 1991 by Richard Lewis. Reprinted by permission of The Touchstone Center for Children, Inc.

"Mother, Mother, I Want Another" by Maria Polushkin Robbins. Copyright © 1978 by Maria Polushkin Robbins. Reprinted by permission of Crown Publishers, Inc.

"If We Didn't Have Birthdays." From HAPPY BIRTHDAY TO YOU! by Dr. Seuss. Copyright © 1959 by Theodor S. Geisel and Audrey S. Geisel, renewed © 1987. Reprinted by permission of Random House, Inc.

"The End." From NOW WE ARE SIX by A. A. Milne. Copyright © 1927 by E. P. Dutton, renewed © 1955 by A. A. Milne. Reprinted by permission of Dutton Children's Books, a division of Penguin Books USA, Inc.

"Good-Bye, Six—Hello, Seven." From IF I WERE IN CHARGE OF THE WORLD AND OTHER WORRIES by Judith Viorst. Copyright © 1981 by Judith Viorst. Reprinted by permission of Atheneum Publishers, an imprint of Macmillan Publishing Company.

"For Someone on His Tenth Birthday." From THE MONSTER DEN by John Ciardi. Copyright © 1963, 1964, 1966, Lippincott. Reprinted by permission of Judith H. Ciardi.

"A Day When Frogs Wear Shoes." From MORE STORIES JULIAN TELLS by Ann Cameron. Copyright © 1986 by Ann Cameron. Reprinted by permission of Alfred A. Knopf, Inc.

"School Is All Over" by Alice Low. Copyright © 1989 by Alice Low. Reprinted by permission of the author.

"What Shall I Pack in the Box Marked 'Summer'?" by Bobbi Katz. Copyright © 1970 by Bobbi Katz. Reprinted by permission of the author.

"Vacation" from FATHERS, MOTHERS, SISTERS, BROTHERS by Mary Ann Hoberman. Copyright © 1991 by Mary Ann Hoberman. Reprinted by permission of Gina Maccoby Literary Agency.

"If Once You Have Slept on an Island." From TAXIS AND TOADSTOOLS by Rachel Field. Copyright © 1926 by The Century Company. Reprinted by permission of Doubleday, a division of Bantam Doubleday Dell Publishing Group, Inc.

"Fireworks," originally titled "Fourth of July Night." From HOP, SKIP AND JUMP by Dorothy Aldis. Copyright © 1934, renewed © 1961 by Dorothy Aldis. Reprinted by permission of G.P. Putnam's Sons.

"And My Heart Soars" by Chief Dan George. Copyright © 1974 by Chief Dan George and Helmut Hirnschall. Reprinted by permission of Hancock House Publishing Ltd.

"Caddie's Independence Day" originally titled "Be Jubilant, My Feet!" From MAGICAL MELONS, MORE STORIES ABOUT CADDIE WOODLAWN by Carol Ryrie Brink. Copyright © 1939, 1940, 1944 by Macmillan Publishing Company, renewed © 1967, 1968, 1972 by Carol Ryrie Brink. Abridged; reprinted by permission of Macmillan Publishing Company.

"Neighbors." From HELLO AND GOODBYE by Mary Ann Hoberman. Copyright © 1959, renewed © 1987 by Mary Ann Hoberman. Reprinted by permission of Gina Maccoby Literary Agency.

"The Opposite of Two." From OPPOSITES by Richard Wilbur. Copyright © 1973 by Richard Wilbur. Reprinted by permission of Harcourt Brace Jovanovich, Inc.

"Since Hanna Moved Away." From IF I WERE IN CHARGE OF THE WORLD AND OTHER WORRIES by Judith Viorst. Copyright © 1981 by Judith Viorst. Reprinted by permission of Atheneum Publishers, an imprint of Macmillan Publishing Company.

"Teddy Gets a Job." From SUPER, DUPER TEDDY by Johanna Hurwitz. Copyright © 1980 by William Morrow. Abridged; reprinted by permission of William Morrow & Company, Inc.

"Summer Goes." From EGG THOUGHTS AND OTHER FRANCES SONGS by Russell Hoban. Copyright © 1964, 1974 by Russell Hoban. Reprinted by permission of HarperCollins Publishers.

"The First Day of School." From RAMONA QUIMBY, AGE 8 by Beverly Cleary. Copyright © 1981 William Morrow. Abridged; reprinted by permission of William Morrow & Company.

"Grandmother Takes Over," originally titled "Mother's Holiday." From MORE TALES OF OLIVER PIG by Jean Van Leeuwen. Copyright © 1981. Reprinted by permission of Penguin U.S.A.

"Some Things About Grandpas." Excerpt from GRANDMAS AND GRANDPAS by Alice Low. Published by Random House, Inc. Copyright © 1962 by Alice Low, © renewed 1990. Reprinted by permission of the author.

"Rosh Ha-shanah Eve" by Harry Philip. From POEMS FOR JEWISH HOLIDAYS. Selected by Myra Cohn Livingston. Copyright © 1986 by Harry Philip. Reprinted by permission of Richard J. Margolis.

"The Witch! The Witch!" From ELEANOR FARJEON'S POEMS FOR CHILDREN. Originally appeared in *Joan's Door* by Eleanor Farjeon. Copyright © 1926, renewed © 1954 by Eleanor Farjeon. Reprinted by permission of HarperCollins Publishers.

"Witch Goes Shopping." From SEE MY LOVELY POISON IVY, by Lilian Moore. Copyright © 1975 by Lilian Moore. Reprinted by permission of Marian Reiner for the author.

"The Birds' Peace" by Jean Craighead George. From THE BIG BOOK FOR PEACE. Copyright © 1990 by Jean Craighead George. Reprinted by permission of Curtis Brown, Ltd.

"The Reason I Like Chocolate." From VACATION TIME by Nikki Giovanni. Copyright © 1980 William Morrow. Reprinted by permission of William Morrow & Company, Inc.

"Hello Book!" by N. M. Bodecker. Copyright © 1978 by N. M. Bodecker; © 1990 by Tumbledown Editions. Reprinted by permission of Tumbledown Editions.

"Keep a Poem in Your Pocket." From SOMETHING SPECIAL by Beatrice Schenk de Regniers. Copyright © 1958, 1986 by Beatrice Schenk de Regniers. Reprinted by permission of Marian Reiner for the author.

"Thanksgiving." From CHERRY STONES! GARDEN SWINGS by Ivy O. Eastwick. Copyright © 1962, renewed © 1990 by Roger Keen. Reprinted by permission of Abingdon Press.

"The First Thanksgiving." From IT'S THANKSGIVING by Jack Prelutsky. Copyright © 1982 by Jack Prelutsky. Reprinted by permission of Greenwillow Books, William Morrow & Company, Inc.

"Thanksgiving" and "Christmas." From AROUND AND ABOUT by Marchette Chute. Copyright © 1957 by E. P. Dutton, renewed © 1985 by Marchette Chute. Reprinted by permission of Mary Chute Smith.

"Potato Pancakes All Around" by Marilyn Hirsh. Copyright © 1978. Reprinted by permission of the Jewish Publication Society.

"Dear Santa Claus." From IT'S CHRISTMAS by Jack Prelutsky. Copyright © 1981 by Jack Prelutsky. Reprinted by permission of Greenwillow Books, William Morrow & Company, Inc.

"Mr. Edwards Meets Santa Claus" from LITTLE HOUSE ON THE PRAIRIE by Laura Ingalls Wilder. Copyright © 1935. Reprinted by permission of HarperCollins Publishers.

"Watch," originally titled Poem 52 (Village). From "Pureza (1912)" in THREE HUNDRED POEMS, 1903–1953 by Juan Ramón Jiménez, translated by Eloise Roach. Copyright © 1962 by Francisco H. Pinzón Jiménez, University of Texas Press. Reprinted by permission of the University of Texas Press.

"Oh Calendar" by J. Patrick Lewis from NEW YEAR'S POEMS. Copyright © 1987 by J. Patrick Lewis. Reprinted by permission of the author.

All titles not listed above are in public domain and are reprinted in various works.

154

Franklin Pierce College Library

00039706

F

Franklin Pierce College Library

00039706